D0603142

# Oman

# Oman

BY LEILA MERRELL FOSTER

*Enchantment of the World*
*Second Series*

Children's Press®

*A Division of Grolier Publishing*

New York   London   Hong Kong   Sydney
Danbury, Connecticut

**Frontispiece:** The incense burner monument, Muscat

*Please note: All statistics are as up-to-date as possible at the time of publication.*

Visit Children's Press on the Internet: http://publishing.grolier.com

Book Production by Herman Adler Design Group

Library of Congress Cataloging-in-Publication Data

Foster, Leila Merrell.
    Oman / by Leila Merrell Foster.
        p.  cm. — (Enchantment of the world.  Second series)
    Includes bibliographical references and index.
    Summary: Describes the geography, plants and animals, history,
economy, language, religions, culture, and people of Oman, a small
nation strategically located on the eastern part of the Arabian
peninsula.
    ISBN 0-516-20964-7
    1. Oman—Juvenile literature. [1. Oman.] I. Title.
II. Series.
DS247.062F67  1999
915.353—dc21                                              98-19572
                                                              CIP
                                                               AC

# Oman

# Contents

**Cover photo:**
The *falaj* irrigation
system

A street scene

A young Omani girl

# Ancient Trade Routes

Ubar, a marvelous city of towers and wealth, was part of an ancient caravan route across a great desert. Caravans carrying frankincense stopped at Ubar to replenish their water supplies and spend the night in safety behind its walls. Frankincense, a fragrant and valuable gum from trees grown in Oman, was used in religious ceremonies in ancient Egypt and other Mediterranean countries.

U BAR IS MENTIONED IN THE KORAN, THE HOLY BOOK OF Islam, and the *Arabian Nights*, which includes the adventures of Aladdin and Sinbad. Claudius Ptolemy, a second-century Egyptian astronomer and geographer, said Ubar was located in the southern desert of Arabia.

*Opposite:* **Pages from a Koran, showing classical Arabic written text**

## A Lost City

Until recently, nobody knew where Ubar or other desert trade routes were located. The vast Empty Quarter (the *Rub' al-Khali*) of the Arabian desert, where the city was said to stand, revealed nothing. In the Empty Quarter, sand dunes reach heights of 600 feet (183 m). Temperatures vary from bitter cold nights to scorching 135°F (57°C) days. Even compasses do not always give accurate readings there. It seemed that the sands had simply swallowed up the city. According to the Koran, Ubar was doomed because of the sins of its residents.

In the early part of the twentieth century, some famous explorers—T. E. Lawrence (better known as

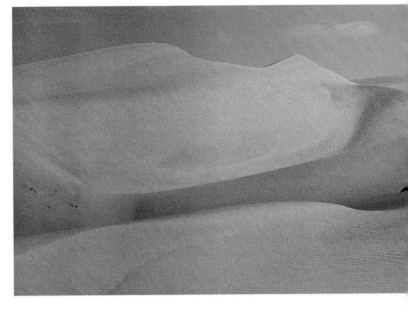

**The Rub' al-Khali (Empty Quarter) sand dunes**

Lawrence of Arabia) and Bertram Thomas—tried to discover where the city was located. They had no luck. Then in 1992, George Hedges, a lawyer with an archaeological background, and Nicholas Clapp, a documentary filmmaker, tackled the problem with some very modern equipment. They enlisted the help of the U.S. Jet Propulsion Laboratory, which supplied them with infrared photos taken from the NASA space shuttle and other satellite photos. By using complex computer programs, they were able to find the traces of old roads in these photos.

Hedges and Clapp then assembled a team to try to locate the city. Archaeologist Juris Zarins of Southwest Missouri State University and British explorer Sir Ranulph Fiennes

**The lost city of Ubar**

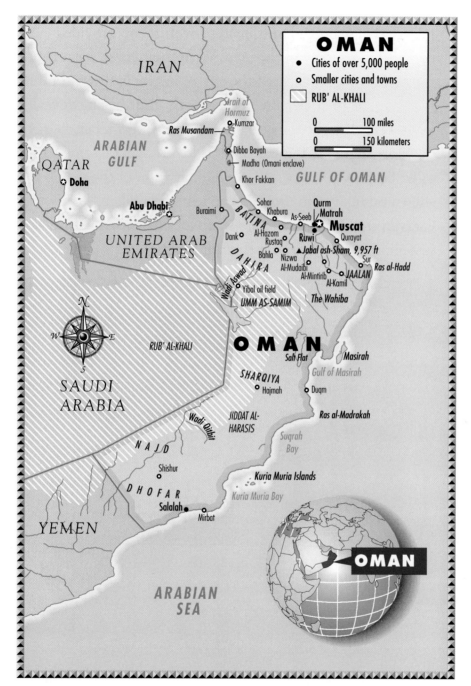

Geopolitical map
of Oman

joined the search. The Omani government provided helicopters for a survey of the area. With the help of local tribes, the archaeologists located the site of an ancient city. Pottery found there included incense burners, and digging revealed what were thought to be the ancient towers of Ubar.

More than 4,000 items have been discovered, some dating as far back as 5000 B.C. A documentary film of the search was shown on television. But did the team find Ubar—or another caravan stop? Is the marvelous city of Ubar with its treasures just another tale from the *Arabian Nights*?

**Tim Severin's *Sohar***

## The Voyage of the Sohar

In 1980, in celebration of the tenth anniversary of the reign of Sultan Qaboos bin Said, a replica of a traditional Omani sailing ship was built and launched on a voyage to China. The ship was named the *Sohar*, after an ancient Omani seaport.

A modern-day seafarer from Ireland named Tim Severin approached the Omanis. He previously had sailed a boat along a route followed by an early Irish explorer. Now, he wanted to follow the route made famous by Omani sailors long ago, by reenacting the voyage of Sinbad.

The replica was built by Omanis in 165 days. The 87-foot (27-m)-long ship was constructed with no nails. Instead, the planks were sewn together in the traditional Omani style. The ship had two settee sails and a jib. The *Sohar* was launched from Oman in November 1980. It arrived in Guangzhou, China, on July 11, 1981, after a voyage that covered some 6,000 miles (9,656 km).

Oman dominated the world of maritime trade long ago, when Omanis sailed the seas in their dhows—traditional Arab boats. The successful voyage of the *Sohar* gives us a glimpse into the life of the Omani sailors in the days of the sailing ships, and the skills they needed to travel the world. It also demonstrates the craftsmanship of today's Omani boat-builders.

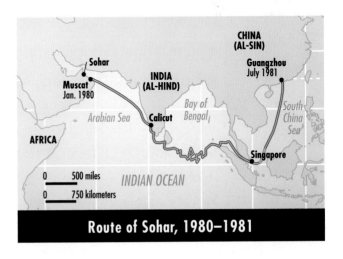

Route of Sohar, 1980–1981

# Strategic Location

The lost city of Ubar had an important location in relation to the land and sea. It stood on a major east–west trade route for frankincense. Later, as Europeans developed their colonial empires, Oman was a source of fresh water on the route to India. Today, Oman's location is important in terms of world trade and world politics because the country lies on the sea routes to rich oil fields.

OMAN IS ON THE EASTERN PART OF THE ARABIAN Peninsula. Its northern tip lies on the Musandam Peninsula overlooking the Strait of Hormuz—an important waterway for the transportation of oil. This part of Oman is separated from the major part of the country by another nation, the United Arab Emirates. The coastal cities along the Arabian Sea offer ports where ships renew their supplies. In the days of sailing ships, the prevailing winds favored trade with Africa, India, and the Spice Islands.

*Opposite:* **The coast of the Musandam Peninsula**

Oman is also renowned for its scenic beauty—its sand, sea, and mountains. It is known for its desert tribes, its sailors, and the variety of people who came to this trading nation over the centuries.

## Land and Sea

Oman is estimated to cover an area of 119,507 square miles (309,500 sq km). The country is larger than Arizona but smaller than New Mexico. Oman borders Saudi Arabia to the west, the United Arab Emirates to the north, and Yemen to the southwest. Some of the borders lie in uninhabited territory. The borders with Yemen and Saudi Arabia were settled in 1997 and 1990, respectively.

The Omani coastline of some 1,056 miles (1,700 km) stretches along the Gulf of Oman and the Arabian Sea, giving access to the Indian Ocean. The island of Masirah, off

**A beach in Oman**

the eastern coast, is also part of Oman. The Omani government has allowed the United States to base military equipment there.

## Geographical Features

**Area:** 119,507 square miles (309,500 sq km)

**Population:** 2,265,000 (est. 1997)

**Highest Elevation:** Jabal ash-Sham, 9,957 feet (3,035 m)

**Lowest Point:** Sea level

**Coastline:** 1,056 miles (1,700 km)

**Capital:** Muscat

**Commercial Center:** Matrah

**Climate:** Desert climate that varies from region to region. The coastal areas are hot and humid with temperatures reaching as high as 116°F (47°C). The interior is hot and dry. In the mountainous regions, the climate is milder.

**Average Annual Precipitation:** 1.5–3.5 inches (4–9 cm) except in the Dhofar region, which receives up to 25 inches (63.5 cm). Oman has no permanent rivers or freshwater lakes.

The Nakal Hot Springs form a stream that is popular for family outings.

## A Hot Climate

According to fourteenth-century geographer Abdul Razak, "The heat . . . was so intense that it burned the marrow in the bones, the sword in its scabbard melted into wax and the gems which adorned the handle of the dagger were reduced to coal.

In the plains the chase became a matter of perfect ease for the desert was strewn with roasted gazelles."

Abdul Razak may have exaggerated, but there is no question that summer in Oman is hot and, along the coastline, humid. Other visitors have reported that Omanis cooked fish on the rocks near Muscat in summer. Before air conditioning, when the hot wind blew off the desert, people slept on their roofs with sheets covering them. During the night, someone sprinkled them with a watering can. The evaporation of the water helped to cool them off.

In summer, at the capital city of Muscat, the temperatures often reach 110°F (43°C) with high humidity. Winters are mild, with lows around 63°F (17°C). Relative humidity in Muscat ranges from 94 percent in July to 20 percent in May. Temperatures in the interior can be even higher, but the air is much drier.

## Rainfall

In Oman, rainfall varies. Two air masses, one from the Mediterranean and the other from the Indian Ocean, bring rain to Oman when the wind currents are right. Annual rainfall averages 1.5–3.5 inches (4–9 cm), but varies greatly in different parts of the country. The Dhofar region receives as much as 25 inches (63.5 cm) in a year.

When several inches of rain fall in arid areas, causing previously dry river beds to overflow, death and destruction result. In 1890, about 700 people were killed in a flash flood when 11.24 inches (28.5 cm) of rain fell in one day.

## The Look of the Land

**Buildings with windtowers, which are used for cooling during the hot season.**

Oman's landscape has a little bit of everything—high mountains, flat plains, deserts, oases, sandy beaches, tall cliffs, and rolling, green hills. The Arabs think of the Hajar mountain

range as a backbone. This range stretches 400 miles (644 km) from Ras ("Cape") Musandam to Ras al-Hadd. They call the area on the Gulf of Oman the *Batina*, meaning "stomach." The area to the west is called the *Dahira*, or "back."

The name of the peninsula at the northern tip, *Musandam*, means "anvil," for the way the waves beat along the coast. This subtropical area has a jagged, fjordlike coastline, similar to parts of Norway.

The Hajar mountain range is the main feature of northern Oman. Jabal ash-Sham, the "Mountain of the Sun," is the highest peak at 9,957 feet (3,035 m).

The coastline of the Batina was built up from debris washed down from the many wadis (streambeds that are dry for much of the year) leading out of the mountains. The coastal plain is the main agricultural and date-growing area. Irrigation water comes from wells that draw off the underground water that runs down from the hills. Without cultivation, only thorny acacias and other hardy desert plants would grow in the area. After a rain, grasses and other herbs sprout from seeds that lie dormant without water.

**Topographical map of Oman**

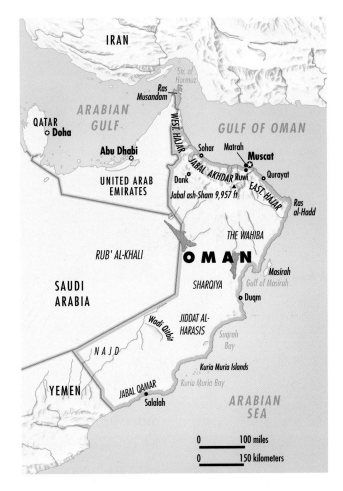

A *falaj* irrigation canal

The Dahira plain on the other side of the mountains was also built up from material washed down from the mountains. Humans have built water channels called *aflaj* (the singular form is *falaj*) to bring the water down from the hills. At the outer limits, the desert takes over, leading into the *Rub' al-Khali*—the Empty Quarter—the great sand desert of Arabia with its huge dunes.

A number of large wadis divide the mountain range from the desert to the sea. The largest of these is the Wadi Samail, which is regarded as the major divide. The geographical areas of northern Oman provided some natural boundaries for five of the ancient governments: Batina, Sharqiya, Dahira, Sir, and al Jauf.

To the south is a wedge-shaped sand area, the Wahiba, about 100 miles (161 km) long and 50 miles (80 km) wide. Dunes of about 200 feet (61 m) in height are rusty-red at their base and honey-colored at the top. The well at Tawi Harian is important because water is scarce for those who cross this area.

**This dam at the top of a dry wadi is intended to prevent flash flooding.**

West of the Wahiba, a gravel plain about 150 miles (241 km) wide is marked by wadis running north to south. West of the wadis and south of the Yibal oil field is a large area of quicksand, Umm as-Samim. This area lies on the border with Saudi Arabia. People and goats have been sucked under and killed by the quicksand. Only a few local tribespeople know the safe routes across this treacherous territory.

Back along the coastline, southwest of the island of Masirah is a flat gravel plain, or steppe, with a few waterholes. One of them, the Umm as-Shadid, is 36 fathoms deep, and according to a local legend was made by a falling star. Before it was overhunted, this area was home to gazelles, oryx, and lizards.

**Graves at Wadi Ghadun**

North of the mountainous region of Dhofar, this steppe merges into a plain called Najd. The finest frankincense came from this region and made Dhofar famous. The ancient city of Ubar is said to lie just north of this area. An old camel route lay through this territory. Traditions claim the city once belonged to the ancient Arabian tribe of Ad, who abandoned it when the water supply failed.

Geodes—hollow stones lined with crystals—are found in the deserts of northern Dhofar, and the mountain ranges contain copper, asbestos, manganese, and salt. Copper was mined even in ancient times. The mountain range of Dhofar begins south of Najd, and runs to the border with Yemen. The range, a continuous chain, has three names for different sections. It is 120 miles (193 km) long but only 20 miles (32 km) wide.

A Beit Kathiri tribesman and his camel rest in the shade of a frankincense tree in the desert.

## Climate Affects Land

Because the southern part of Oman catches the southwest monsoon rains, it is covered with green vegetation that from November onward turns yellow. The high mountains, some up to 5,000 feet (1,524 m), cause the rain to fall here. While the southern side is green or yellow, the northern side is almost bare—without vegetation.

## Oman's Key Cities

Matrah, the largest city, is located on the Gulf of Oman, just west of Muscat, the capital. Matrah has one of the busiest and most modern ports in the region, Mina Qaboos, named after the sultan. Matrah also has the biggest souk, or market, in the area.

The city of Nizwa was the capital of Oman in the sixth and seventh centuries. Today it is one of the most popular tourist attractions because of its historical buildings and seventeenth-century fort. It is also famous for its busy souk, where visitors can buy silver and copper jewelry.

Salalah (left), the capital city of the Dhofar region, has many coconut plantations. In addition, bananas, papaya, wheat, and sugarcane are grown here. Salalah has a port at Rasut, a fishing center for sardines, crayfish, and lobster.

The narrow coastal plain in the south is about 30 miles (48 km) long, but its only 5 miles (8 km) wide. Salalah is the capital of this southern region. The plain produces a variety of crops and vegetables.

Date palms are the major crop of northern Oman, while coconut palms grow better in the climate of Dhofar. Along wadis with constantly flowing water, such as Wadi Tiwi, crops are grown on terraces cut into the hillsides.

Salalah is separated from Muscat, the capital, by 600 miles (966 km), by road, of desolate country. Sea travel used to be the best way to travel between the southern and northern parts of Oman. Today, of course, air transportation links them.

The towns along the coast are home to fishers, sailors, and merchants involved in imports and exports and diving for pearls. The towns farther inland are dependent on agriculture and serve as distribution centers for products moving between the coast and the interior.

**A farm in al-Hammam surrounded by date palms**

# Frankincense and Oryx

Have you ever wished that candy grew on trees?
Omani children have sweets that grow on plants.
They eat the leaves of the camel-thorn, knib, or
nabag. When rain falls in the desert, the country
springs to life with flowers in bloom. Oman even has
some Alpine flowers that have survived from the last
Ice Age.

# O

## Plants of Oman

LEANDER, PEACH, APRICOT, AND ALMOND ADD BEAUTY
to the landscape. The yellow and red blooms of the golden
shower tree and the royal poinciana, or flame tree, are seen in
May and October. A tiny wild pansy and cowslip can be
found, as well as small dandelions. The country's varied climate allows many different kinds of plants to grow. One tree,
*Anogeissus dhofarcica*, is abundant in the Dhofar region but
grows nowhere else in the world.

Some of the plants have practical uses. An anesthetic is
made from the thorn apple. Henna, made from the yellow
flowers of another plant, is used by Omani women as a
cosmetic. Cotton plants
and a wild potato are also
found in Oman. Dates are
a popular food, and limes
and other citrus fruits are
also grown. Wild moun-
tain roses are cultivated
for making rosewater.

Sultan Qaboos bin
Said, the ruler of Oman,
has established a number
of nature preserves. In
1990, a new species of
flower was developed and
named after him.

*Opposite:* **A royal poinciana
(flame tree)**

**Henna used as a
cosmetic design**

## Frankincense

This fragrant aromatic gum resin was an important export of Oman in ancient times. Frankincense was used in worship and medicine in the empires of the Mediterranean world. In the Bible, incense is frequently mentioned for use in the sanctuary. One of the gifts that the Wise Men brought to the baby Jesus was frankincense.

Although Western medicine today does not recognize the value of incense, it has been used both internally and externally to treat a wide range of illnesses. At one time, incense was thought to counteract poison. Frankincense is still used in incense, perfumes, and fumigants.

The gum is collected by making cuts in the trunks of frankincense trees. The trees are not tall. They grow to a height of only about 10 to 16 feet (3 to 5 m). A milky liquid, or gum, flows out from the cut in the trunk (below). The liquid hardens when it is exposed to air. The gum is then stripped off, sorted by color (bluish-white is best), and stored before being sent to market. One tree can produce up to 44 pounds (20 kg) per season.

Oman is one of the few countries (along with Yemen and Somalia) where these trees grow. About 2,000 years ago, a Roman historian named Pliny said that the people of south Arabia were the richest people on earth because they controlled the frankincense trade. The product was still providing important income into the sixth century.

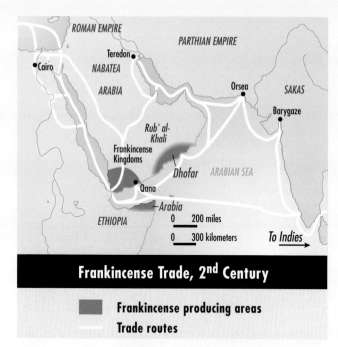

## Frankincense Trade, 2nd Century

▪ Frankincense producing areas

— Trade routes

## Animals in the Wild

Many of Oman's animals have been overhunted for their meat. The oryx—an antelope—and the tahr—a mountain goat—are especially threatened. The tahr lives in high, out-of-the-way places. It is only about 24 inches (61 cm) high. In 1976, the sultan put a ban on hunting the tahr. Although its population has more than doubled since then, the animal is still very rare. The government runs a breeding center for endangered species that they hope to reintroduce into wild habitats.

The Arabian oryx, an antelope with a white coat, has been hunted almost to extinction.

The tahr is a mountain goat that is in danger of becoming extinct.

Foxes, leopards, wild cats, panthers, wolves, and hyenas still survive in parts of Oman. Porcupines, hyrax, hedgehogs, hares, jerboa, gerbils, mice, rats, toads, and bats also live here. Lizards sometimes reach a length of 24 inches (61 cm). The Jabal Akhdar has been set aside as a national park to protect some of these animals.

Locusts sometimes devastate crops. In Oman, however, they also serve as food for Omanis who catch and eat or sell them. Less welcome are the horned viper, a small boa, spiders up to 4 inches (10 cm) long with a painful bite, and centipedes that grow up to 6 inches (15 cm), as well as beetles, flies, mosquitoes, ants, and termites.

Small fish eat debris in wadi pools. Freshwater snails are also numerous. Some farming areas have many beautiful butterflies.

Birds of many species live in Oman or migrate between Africa and Europe and Oman. Falconry, an important sport in other parts of Arabia, is practiced only by the Omanis of the Dahira. Some birds, such as the houbara and the sooty falcon, are protected in Oman.

Domestic animals include cattle, sheep, goats, chicken, dogs (including the saluki), and cats. Dogs and cats are not popular as pets, however. The Omani camels are among the swiftest and most graceful in all Arabia.

**A lanner falcon**

**A boy and a woman with her goat in Khasab**

**Young jockeys participate in a camel race.**

Omani horse breeding and export was noted by Marco Polo in his travels, and horses continued to be an important trade item until recently. The thousands of horses mentioned in historical records suggest that larger areas of the country must once have been cropland in order to supply the food for these animals. Today, fine camels are bred and raised.

The seas near Oman are rich in marine life. The shores are home to crabs and turtles. While oysters are found along the coast, pearling has never been as important as it is in the shallower waters of the Persian, or Arabian, Gulf. However, Muscat has long been an important market for pearls and mother-of-pearl. Several new varieties of seashells have been found on Omani beaches.

Four species of giant turtles come ashore in Oman each year to lay their eggs. They are the loggerhead, the green, the olive ridley, and the hawks-bill. The females come ashore to lay thousands of eggs on the beaches around Ras al-Hadd and Masirah Island. However, only a few baby turtles make it past the foxes and gulls to the safety of the ocean. Those that do may have a life span of some 200 years. Today, the government has set aside protected areas for the giant sea turtles. People who wish to visit these conservation areas must get permission from the Ministry of National Heritage.

**A sea turtle from Ras al-Junais**

### Oryx or Unicorn?

The mythical unicorn has only one horn. Most oryx have two horns but, from a distance, they can look like unicorns. Unfortunately, the wild oryx, a species of white antelope once found in great numbers in Oman, was hunted almost to extinction. It was prized for its meat, and its horn was used as a medicine.

The oryx is 40 to 47 inches (102 to 120 cm) tall at the shoulder. It has a mane, a tufted tail, dark patches on its face and forehead, and dark streaks on each side of its eyes.

Some of the animals raised in captivity have been reintroduced into the wild. Some oryx raised in the Phoenix Zoo and the San Diego Wild Animal Park have been returned to their native habitat in Oman and are guarded from poachers by rangers. These animals run free and are reproducing well.

The oryx were returned to the wild only ten years after the last wild animal was killed and twenty years after the zoo breeding program began. Naturalists believe that this short period of time in captivity increases the survival of the animal in the wild.

# Traders over Time

Oman's history has been influenced by the country's location on important trading routes. For centuries, the Omanis were great traders and controlled the seas, sometimes as the dominant power—and sometimes as pirates.

# A
## Prehistoric Times

ROUND 12,000 B.C., TOWARD THE END OF THE LAST great Ice Age, the people who lived in Oman hunted gazelle, oryx, wild goat, ostrich, and other animals. They also gathered berries and wild fruit, but they had not yet discovered that they could plant and harvest crops.

*Opposite:* **Clusters of flint flakes**

**Fortified watchtowers were used to guard early settlements.**

Oman received more rain and had more vegetation then, so it probably supported more people. Shishur, in Dhofar, was an important center for the production of flints. The tools and weapons of this stone age are of a very high quality.

Judging from the style of jars found in tombs, scientists believe that the people of this region were linked with either Mesopotamia in what is now Iraq or Tepe Yaha in southern Iran. As time went on, these people may have traded with Egypt and even with India. The Omanis have been skilled boatbuilders for a long time. Records from Mesopotamia claim that boats came from a place called Magan bringing wood, diorite, and copper. These products seem to indicate that Magan may have been the land we call Oman.

Over time, Omanis settled down in villages. They lived near wadis from which they obtained water for the wheat they now planted. They built fortified watchtowers, used potter's wheels, wove cloth, and tamed animals to carry them and their heavy loads.

According to Arab historians, the earliest inhabitants of the peninsula were called Al-Ariba. Ancient stories describe heroes of huge stature. Great stone circles in Oman may date from this period of legend. Two of the heroes, Ad and Thamad, provided the names of early Arab tribes. Two sisters, Tasm and Jadis, also gave their names to early tribes, suggesting that the mother's line was more important in tracing relationships. Another story has the Queen of Sheba in south Arabia ruling this area. According to yet another tale, Abdul Shams, who constructed a remarkable sluice dam at Marib in Yemen, was once the ruler of the Omani territory.

## The Age of Empires

Cyrus the Great, founder of Persia's Achaemenid dynasty, conquered Oman in 563 B.C. Another Persian ruler, Darius I, commissioned exploration of the sea routes between India and Egypt.

**Cyrus the Great**

Alexander the Great, the Macedonian who defeated the Persians, was also interested in sea routes. He sent his admiral Nearchus with some 1,500 boats from India in 325 B.C. In his journal, Nearchus mentioned the Cape of Arabia called Maketa (probably Ras Musandam), from which cinnamon and other products were shipped. Alexander's death in 323 cut short further plans for his empire. Gold was an important cargo between the gulf area and Ceylon (now Sri Lanka).

The Roman historian Pliny told about Arab ships that took advantage of the northeast monsoons for trading with India. The ships were guarded by many archers because the area was also frequented by pirates.

## The Coming of Islam

Islam, the religion proclaimed by the prophet Muhammad in Mecca (now in Saudi Arabia) reached Oman about A.D. 630. Many Arab Omanis adopted the new faith.

On the death of Muhammad, his friend Abu Bakr became the caliph—the leader of all those who followed Islam. Sometime between 632 and 634, the caliph's general, Hudhaifa bin Muhsin, won a battle at Dibba and remained in Oman as governor.

The Omanis played an important role in the growth of Islam. In an expedition launched from Omani ports, the Arabs attacked the Persians, who did not embrace Islam as readily. The Arab tribe of Azd fought in the Battle of the Camel between Islamic factions on the side of Aisha,

Muhammad's widow. Though they were defeated, the Azd gained great influence in Basra (in southern Iraq) and were given control over a number of tribal groups.

With the leadership in the hands of their tribe, many Omanis were attracted to Basra. The Omanis made up a large part of the army. They fought in many of the early battles and gained great wealth. Then the caliph turned against the Azd leader. Many Omanis returned to their own country when their troops were defeated.

Conflict between the Omanis and the caliphs continued for some time. As the power of the caliph weakened, Oman began to prosper. Ships were built. Sohar became the greatest seaport in Islam, as Omani ships traded with Africa and Madagascar. Its power attracted enemies, however. Sohar was attacked in 965 and eventually destroyed in 971 by the dynasty that controlled the caliph, then living in Baghdad, in present-day Iraq.

That dynasty did not last long because the Seljuk Turks swept in from the steppes of central Asia and took over Baghdad. By 1064, the Seljuks also occupied Oman.

The next 300 years saw power shifts between religious and political leaders and among three city states that successively took leadership in trade after the fall of Sohar—Siraf, Qais, and Hormuz. When the Portuguese arrived in 1507, their leader wrote that every house in Muscat had a secret cupboard for storing wealth when there was a raid from the interior of the country.

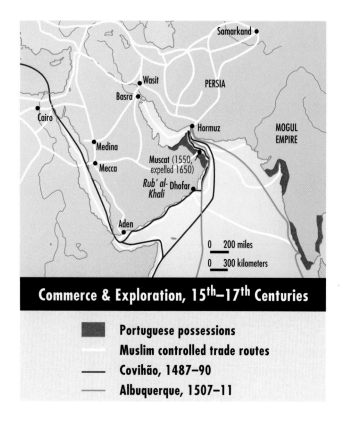

**Commerce & Exploration, 15th–17th Centuries**

- Portuguese possessions
- Muslim controlled trade routes
— Covihão, 1487–90
— Albuquerque, 1507–11

### Ahmad bin Madjid

Vasco da Gama, the Portuguese explorer at the end of the fifteenth century, found a sea route from western Europe to the East by way of the Cape of Good Hope around the tip of Africa. Da Gama hired Omani sailor Ahmad bin Madjid as his pilot to get his ship from Africa across the Indian Ocean to Calicut, on the west coast of India.

## European Interest

The Portuguese arrived first—sailing around the tip of Africa. Vasco da Gama hired an Omani sailor to pilot his ship from east Africa across the Indian Ocean to Calicut, a city on the coast of south India. Alfonso de Albuquerque followed in 1506 with five ships and plans to dominate the Red Sea and the Persian Gulf. He was impressed with the agriculture of Oman, its harbors, and its elegant towns and fine houses. The Portuguese sacked Muscat in 1507 and soon controlled the entire coast. They built forts and took over the collection of custom revenues at Hormuz. The Portuguese retained their power in Oman until 1650.

The Dutch, the English, and the French soon arrived in the rich trading area. These countries competed against one another for local alliances. The Omanis, under leaders that became the Ya'ruba dynasty, were able to drive the Portuguese from their forts. Oman has never been occupied by any other country except from 1737 to 1747, when the Persians became involved in an Omani civil war. Instead, Omanis negotiated treaties of friendship—especially with the British—that allowed them to keep their independence while giving other countries the trading advantages they wanted.

Modern Sohar seaport, on the coast of the Gulf of Oman

Much later, in 1833, Oman entered into a Treaty of Friendship with the United States. In 1836, an Omani ship that docked in New York Harbor attracted the interest of Americans, and later treaties continued the friendship of the two countries. Sultan Qaboos bin Said made a state visit to the United States in 1983, and U.S. vice president George Bush visited Oman in 1984 and 1986.

**A historic Portuguese fort in Muscat**

## The Ya'ruba Dynasty

Oman grew strong under the leaders of the Ya'ruba dynasty. They were able to unify the country and went on to build up the navy and army and encourage trade. They put up elegant buildings and founded colleges that produced famous theologians and scholars.

The first leader, Nasir bin Murshid, was called the "sun of salvation." He came to power in 1624 and brought unity to Oman. At his death, his cousin Sultan bin Saif took over and extended Omani influence abroad. He drove out the Portuguese.

Later leaders brought conflict to the country. One of the sultan's sons, Bil'arub, was nicknamed "the calamity of the Arabs" and his other son, Saif, was called "the scourge." Saif proved to be the stronger in the fight for local control. He attacked the Portuguese in Africa and near India.

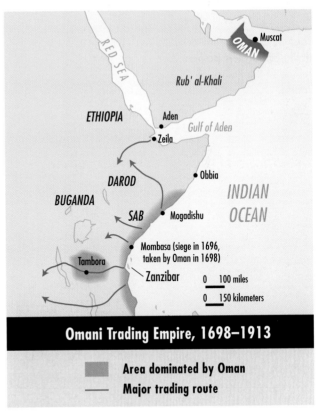

Along with many of the European powers, Saif turned to privateering—attacking cargo ships. He became very wealthy. He owned 700 male slaves and 28 ships including the *al Falak*, which was armed with 90 large guns.

When Saif died in 1711, he was succeeded by his son, Saif II. The son moved his capital from Rustaq to

There is a Persian influence in the elaborately painted ceiling of the Palace of Jabrin.

al-Hazom, where he built a large fort. He spent all his inheritance and borrowed money besides. When he died in 1718, his son was not old enough to govern, and civil war broke out with many challengers for leadership.

The young Saif bin Sultan brought in soldiers from Baluchistan and appealed to the shah of Persia for help. The shah sent a powerful horse to Saif and told him that if he could ride it, the shah would send soldiers. Saif rode the horse furiously through a wadi near Muscat and landed safely on his feet when the horse jumped a wall. Unfortunately, the horse broke a leg and had to be destroyed.

The Persians then sent soldiers to help control the rebels. Saif died in 1743, broken up over the refusal of the Persians to give up the Omani forts. No other members of the family came forward to take over leadership, so the Ya'ruba dynasty came to an end.

## The Said Dynasty

One Omani leader, Ahmad bin Said, continued to fight against the Persians. He succeeded in driving them out and governed his country well. He established the Al Bu Said dynasty, which has ruled Oman ever since.

After Ahmad's death, power was divided between the imam, a religious authority, and the sultan, who had political power. This separation of powers would cause conflict a number of times in later history. A grandson of Ahmad, Said bin Sultan, took back Omani control over Zanzibar—an island off the east coast of Africa—and moved there. When Said died, the empire was split between two sons—one ruling Zanzibar

### Ahmad bin Said and the Persians

Plotting to get rid of the Persians, Ahmad bin Said invited them to a great banquet at Barka. While the Persians were at dinner, it was announced that anyone with a grudge against the Persians could now take revenge. Only 200 Persians survived the massacre that followed. The Persians left Oman, and Ahmad bin Said became a hero and was elected the leader.

Two of Ahmad's sons took over forts in Muscat. When an outsider sought to take advantage of conflict within the family by trying to seize power, the father and sons united to defeat him. Other rivals were made into friends by the arrangement of marriages between the two groups.

After Ahmad had consolidated his power in Oman, he turned to foreign activities. He built up his fleet to thirty-four warships and led 10,000 men against the Persians at Basra. His ship broke the iron chain that was stretched across the river as a defense of that city. The Ottoman sultan who claimed Basra was so pleased by the defeat of the Persians that he paid a subsidy to Oman until 1856. Ahmad also earned the friendship of the Mogul emperor Shah Alam in India because his fleet attacked the pirates that sailed the west coast of India.

Ahmad collected custom revenues, administered his country well, and gave sweets to the children of the poor. He made himself available to the people, but he traveled with much pomp and ceremony. His personal bodyguard included 1,000 free men, 1,000 Zanzibaris, and 100 Nubian slaves. They carried four banners with staffs topped by gold and silver. His court included scholars, tribal leaders, and even executioners.

**The al-Hazam fort at Rustaq**

and continuing the dynasty there until 1964, and the other ruling Oman. When the two sultanates were divided, much of the fleet was based in Zanzibar and was lost to Oman. Oman's fortunes declined greatly due to competition from foreign ships, especially steamships, and the decline of the slave trade.

The dynasty in Oman declined and might have collapsed without the support of the British. It was frequently attacked by imams with a power base in the interior of the country. Finally in 1920, the British negotiated a treaty among the tribal leaders known as the Agreement of al-Sib. Under this treaty, the sultan recognized the interior as self-governing but still part of Oman.

In 1954, a new imam attempted to set up a separate government. He planned to use the possibility of oil discoveries as a financial base and give Saudi Arabia an interest in the territory. Sultan Said bin Taimur, who had assumed power in 1932, met this threat with the help of British military intervention. Ten of the Arab countries, unhappy with the rule in Oman, put the problems of Oman on the United Nations Assembly agenda, over Britain's objections. The movement for separation was finally resolved in 1970 when other countries withdrew their backing of the separatist group.

Meanwhile, in 1968, the Marxist Popular Front for the Liberation of the Occupied Arab Gulf—a communist group—took control of a rebellion in the Dhofar region. They were aided by neighboring South Yemen (then under communist

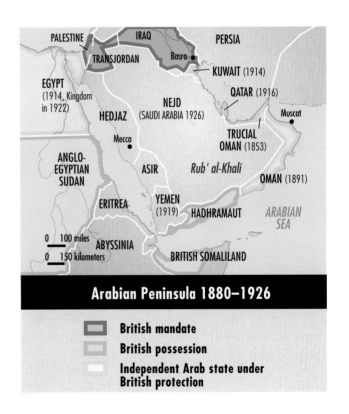

### Arabian Peninsula 1880–1926

- British mandate
- British possession
- Independent Arab state under British protection

**The bombed ruins of Tanuf**

control) and received assistance from the People's Republic of China and the Soviet Union that included such weapons as SAM-7 missiles. People were unhappy with the sultan's cautious spending of the oil revenues that had come to Oman by 1967. In addition, the sultan had isolated himself from his people.

## Sunken Treasure

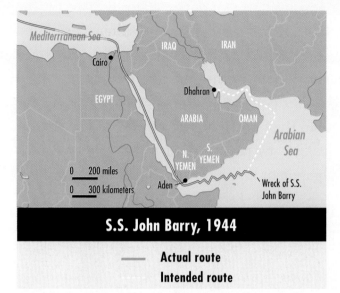

**S.S. John Barry, 1944**

—— **Actual route**
**Intended route**

Lost treasure is not always buried under sand and debris, like the ancient city of Ubar. Sometimes it lies at the bottom of the sea, and sometimes it is not so ancient. In 1944, during World War II (1939–1945), the United States minted 3 million silver coins in Philadelphia at the request of the government of Saudi Arabia. The coins were shipped aboard the Liberty ship SS *John Barry*. The ship's destination was Dhahran, in the eastern province of Saudi Arabia. The money would be used to pay construction workers in the oil fields. Oil had been discovered there only six years earlier, and the United States needed oil for its war effort.

German submarines torpedoed the *John Barry* in the Arabian Sea more than 100 nautical miles (185 km) off the coast of Oman. The Liberty ship broke in two and sank in 8,500 feet (2,600 m) of water.

Rumors circulated that the ship's cargo included not only coins, but also silver bullion—bars of silver. Published accounts of a report by the ship's captain set a value of U.S.$26 million on the silver bullion, which now lay in very deep water. The value of the silver in the coins was U.S.$540,000, and the face value of the coins was about U.S.$900,000—nowhere near the claim of U.S.$26 million.

Salvage rights to the ship were advertised by the United States in 1987. If all the claims about the cargo were correct, by 1987 the treasure would have been worth U.S.$380 million. But if the cargo consisted of only the coins, their value would not pay for the salvaging costs. Two Americans won the salvage rights with a bid of $50,010.

There was a legal problem because the wreckage was off the shore of Oman, although it was not in Omani waters. Fortunately, an Omani businessman and a British salvage expert organized a group to dive for the cargo. By 1992, they had found the wreckage but, given its position in such deep water, recovery would be difficult.

Finally, in 1994, the first glimmer of the silver coins appeared. Some 1.3 million Saudi coins weighing 17 tons were recovered. The rest of the coins had to be abandoned. Where was the bullion? It has not yet been found. The salvaged coins have been offered for sale in the United States.

The Dhofar uprising was one of the major reasons for the palace coup of July 23, 1970, in which the sultan was ousted by his son, Qaboos bin Said. Qaboos had trained at the Royal Military Academy, Sandhurst, in Great Britain. He reversed his father's isolationist policy, and Oman was admitted to the Arab League and to the United Nations in 1971. The Dhofar uprising was put down by late 1975 with the help of British personnel and equipment and Jordanian and Iranian troops.

**The site of the 1975 recapture of Dalkhut**

Sultan Qaboos set about establishing a cabinet and a modern government. Oman was one of six founding members of the Gulf Cooperation Council, a group designed to promote cooperation among the Gulf nations. Oman tried to stay neutral during the Iran-Iraq War of 1980–1988. However, when Iraq invaded Kuwait in 1990, the sultan permitted Western troops to be based in Oman. An Omani regiment took part in the liberation of Kuwait in February 1991.

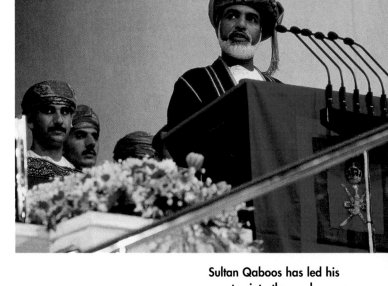

Sultan Qaboos has led his country into the modern era.

In 1994, the sultan was faced with another uprising, this time under the guise of Islamic reforms. However, its leaders were quickly arrested for treason. In 1995, Qaboos celebrated twenty-five years in power with a tour designed to cement relations with the tribes of the interior of the country. He has also worked at developing economic stability that does not rely so heavily on oil revenues and at improving government.

## Sultan Said bin Taimur

Sultan Said bin Taimur ruled from 1932 until 1970. Born in 1910, he assumed his rule on the abdication of his father. He was a devout Muslim and spoke and read English well. He did not spend money on fancy cars and yachts, but preferred the simpler life. He was a good sportsman and drove his own desert jeeps and trucks.

His conservative policy of isolating Oman from foreign influences followed that of some other leaders in the Arabian Peninsula. He feared what might happen to traditional Omani culture and religion if outsiders were allowed to influence the country. However, his tight controls resulted in rebellion from Omanis who wanted to benefit from oil revenues and modernization. When his son ousted him in 1970, Taimur went to live in London. He died there in 1972.

# The Modern Sultanate

Oman has had a long history, at times as a world power. Bad experiences with foreign occupation and influence, however, made some sultans wary of out-side pressures. During the reign of Sultan Said bin Taimur, which ended in 1970, radios, bicycles, and sunglasses were banned in Muscat. Electricity was rationed, and the city gates were locked at sundown.

OMAN WAS A VERY POOR COUNTRY AT THAT TIME. Public notices were posted on a bulletin board outside the palace. Oil, which was discovered in 1964, had not yet begun to bring in substantial revenues. Even slavery was tolerated if there was an economic advantage. This was the base from which Sultan Qaboos bin Said in 1970 had to form a government and try to raise the people's living conditions.

*Opposite:* **A modern four-lane highway in Muscat**

## Flag of Oman

Three equal horizontal stripes of white, red, and green, to the right of a red vertical stripe, decorate the Omani flag. The white stands for peace and prosperity; the red, for Omani blood; and the green, for Islam and for the fertility of the land. Before 1970, the flag was all red. The national emblem is at the top of the red vertical stripe. It is a *khanjar*, a curved dagger, in its scabbard superimposed on two crossed swords in scabbards. The emblem also appears on the nation's currency.

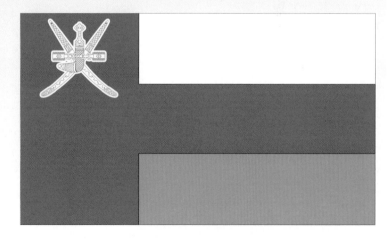

## *The Power of the Sultan*

The sultan has absolute power. Oman has no written constitution. However, since the sultan formalized the structures of government in a public law, some writers think Oman can be classed as a constitutional monarchy.

The sultan receives assistance from a Council of Ministers who may make decisions in his absence. The country has no legislature but, instead, a Consultative Council, called the *Majlis ash-Shoura.* In late 1996, plans were announced for a Council of State, called the *Majlis ad-Dawlah*, which, along with the Consultative Council, would act as a liaison between the government and the people.

### NATIONAL GOVERNMENT OF OMAN

Head of State

Sultan

Executive

Sultan, who can delegate authority to the Council of Ministers

Legislative

Sultan, who can obtain help from the Consultative Council (Majlis ash-Shoura) and the Council of State (Majlis ad-Dawlah)

Judicial

Traditional Islamic judges with a newly established Supreme Court to interpret the law

**Sultan Qaboos Speaks to the People of Oman**

"I promise to you to proceed forthwith in the process of creating a modern government. My first act will be the immediate abolition of all unnecessary restrictions on your lives and activities. . . . I will proceed as quickly as possible to transform your life into a prosperous and bright future. Every one of you must play his part towards this goal. Our country in the past was famous and strong. . . . Yesterday it was complete darkness and with the help of God, tomorrow will be a new dawn on Muscat, Oman, and its people."

—Speech delivered July 23, 1970, on his ascent to power

The Consultative Council is made up of 80 members (one for each region with fewer than 30,000 persons and two for areas with 30,000 or more persons). The sultan appoints the members from lists of two or, in the case of the larger regions, four candidates. In 1995, women were allowed to run for this council, and four women were elected in the first round of voting. Members serve a three-year term of office and can propose legislation. They are guaranteed free speech except for criticism of the sultan.

**The buildings and grounds of Oman's Consultative Council, the *Majlis ash-Shoura***

Government officials may not belong to this council. When the officials appeared before the council in televised sessions, public criticism of the government was humiliating to some of the officials. As a result, government officials have denied information to the council, thereby undercutting its effectiveness.

The Council of State is made up of prominent Omanis appointed by the sultan. This group is supposed to be a liaison between the government and the people.

H.E. Abdulla bin Ali al-Qatabi, president of the Consultative Council

Sultan Qaboos is not only the head of state but also the prime minister and the minister of foreign affairs, defense, and finance. Recently the sultan proclaimed, as public law, a system for who would succeed him. He gets to name the person from the royal family unless the royal family agrees on another candidate within three days of his death.

The new Basic Law of 1996 provides a bill of rights guaranteeing freedom of the press, religious tolerance, and equality of race and gender. These rights are unprecedented among nations in the Gulf area. Some critics doubt that the Basic Law will be fully established by the target date of 2000.

## Sultan Qaboos bin Said

Sultan Qaboos was born on November 18, 1940. That day is now a national holiday in Oman. As a child, Qaboos was isolated in the royal palace. His father allowed him no servants and told him that he had to work or starve. He was no better than other Omanis.

The father's British advisers urged the sultan to send his son abroad for further education. Reluctantly, the father let his son go first to a private school in England and then on to Britain's Royal Military Academy, Sandhurst.

When Qaboos returned to Oman, his more liberal ideas clashed with his father's. He remained within the palace at Salalah under house arrest for the next six years. During this time he studied the Koran and the teachings of the Ibadhi faith of Islam.

After careful planning, and with the support of the British, Qaboos asked his father to step down and give him control of the government. This change in power was nonviolent. The father left for London, where he died two years later.

The task that faced Qaboos was immense, and he was only thirty years old at the time. He began with projects involving housing and public services, followed by electricity and water, then health and education. The oil money that started coming in had to be used wisely. It was also necessary to plan for economic growth that did not rely entirely on oil.

Qaboos has demonstrated his independence in foreign affairs. He has maintained good relations with the post-revolutionary Islamic government of Iran and with Egypt, which

**The construction of a new seawall along the coast of Oman**

signed a peace accord with Israel. In 1994, he welcomed Israeli prime minister Yitzak Rabin for a brief visit. However, Oman's relations with Israel have cooled with the breakdown of the peace process between the Israeli government and the Palestinian Authority in Israel.

The sultan wants to maintain Oman's traditional character as much as possible and has worked to preserve historic buildings and sections. He has been cautious about introducing tourism for the same reason. Also, he has helped preserve Oman's plants and animals.

Every year, the sultan tours areas of his country to meet the people. He often drives to a town in the interior to discuss a local issue with officials there. He has won the respect of many of his people. However, some Omanis fear that officials are now isolating the sultan from the people. They claim that officials who control access to the sultan are turning his annual tours of the country into mere formalities.

Sultan Qaboos enjoys classical music and reading about military history. His favorite sport is horseback riding.

## The Judicial System

Courts apply Islamic law primarily to personal cases involving family and inheritance. A civil court system based on English common law deals with other matters. Judges are appointed to the local courts by the Minister of Justice and Religious Endowments and Islamic Affairs. Appeals from the local courts go to the Court of Appeal in the capital city of Muscat. In

### Muscat: Did You Know This?

Muscat and its modern suburbs are called the capital area. This area is a thriving district that includes a deepwater port, an oil tanker loading zone, military bases, and Seeb International Airport.

**Population:** 51,969

**Average summer temperature:** 90°F (32°C)

**Average winter temperature:** 60–74°F (15–23°C)

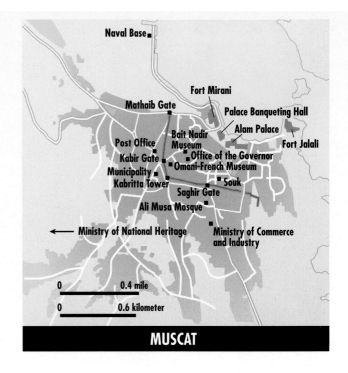

1987, the Omanis established a "flying court" to serve remote areas. The newly established Supreme Court interprets the law.

### Local Government

Eight local governorates divide the country: Muscat, al-Batina, Musandam, adh-Dahira, ad-Dakhiya, ash-Sharqiya, al-Wosta, and Dhofar. Muscat, the capital, is the most densely populated; al-Wosta has the smallest population.

**An Omani helicopter pilot**

### Oman's Armed Forces

In 1996, Oman's army had 25,000 men; the navy, 4,200; the air force, 4,100; and the royal household, 6,500. Service is voluntary. Defense spending was estimated at 32.5 percent of total expenditures for that year.

### Social Welfare and Education

Great advances have been made since 1970. Today, Oman has free health services, forty-six hospitals, and eighty-two health centers. Citizens of other member states of the Gulf Cooperation Council are eligible to receive the same medical services as Omanis. In 1994, health care accounted for 6.4 percent of the nation's expenditures, with another 3.2 percent spent on social security and welfare.

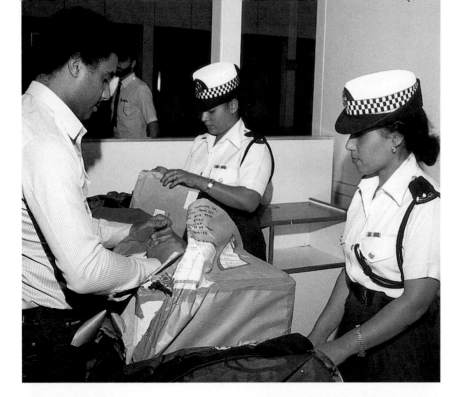

Female customs
police officers

Great advances have
been made in Omani
health services.

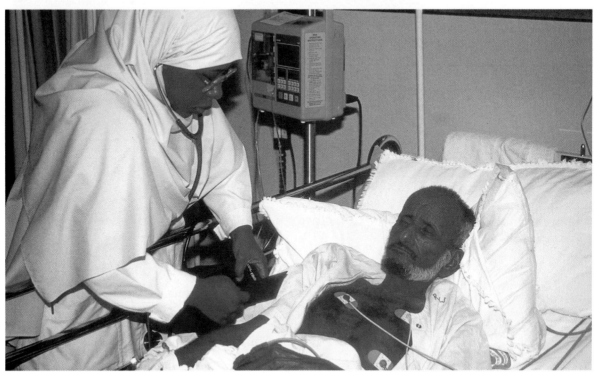

**A kindergarten teacher and her student in Muscat**

Education is not compulsory but it is free. Primary school begins at six years of age and lasts for six years. The next level is divided into preparatory and secondary and lasts for another six years. Enrollment has been increasing, and by 1993 an estimated 85 percent of primary-school-age children were in school and 61 percent of eligible children attended preparatory and secondary classes. Teacher-training colleges and technical institutes have also been established. There are eight Islamic colleges. The first national university, named after Sultan Qaboos, was opened in 1986 and by 1995 had 4,296 students. In 1970, 80 percent of the adult population was considered illiterate. With adult classes, over 59 percent of the adult population are now literate. Literacy among males is about twice as high as among females.

School enrollment has been increasing in recent years.

A biology student at Sultan Qaboos University

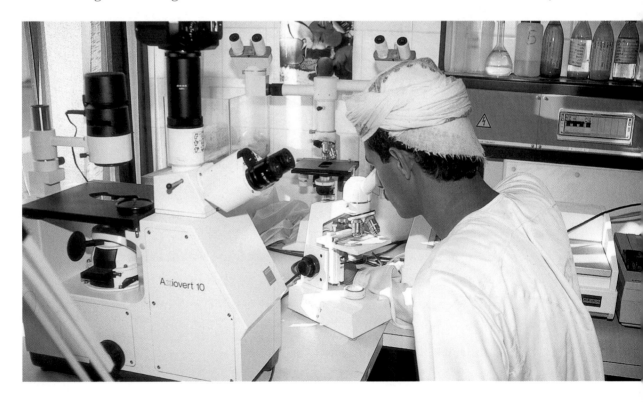

# Oil Wealth and Economic Development

Oil fuels the economic development of Oman, but the government is encouraging establishment of other industries. If the country can build up other industries, its economy will be more stable.

THE FIRST COMMERCIAL PRODUCTION OF OIL CAME IN 1967, but it was not until 1970 that the revenues from oil were used to expand the economy. Because Oman's oil reserves are small in comparison with other Arabian countries, the government does not want to become too dependent on this resource. Oman wants to diversify its economy—to find a variety of ways to make money.

### The Petroleum and Natural Gas Industry

In recent years, as much as 90 percent of the government revenue came from oil and natural gas. The sale of crude

A truck moving a large natural gas tank

petroleum and natural gas amounted to 36 percent of the nation's income. In short, this industry is very important.

When prices in the oil industry fall, the government has to delay some of its plans. Because Oman is not a member of the Organization of Petroleum Exporting Countries (OPEC) or the Organization of Arab Petroleum Exporting Countries (OAPEC), which control production and pricing, it has been able to make up for price declines with increased production. However, Oman is sensitive to OPEC actions and has voluntarily decreased production at times to help stabilize international prices.

The two main areas of production are the central oil fields southwest of Muscat and the southern oil fields in Dhofar. Pipelines carry the oil to the port of Mina al-Fahal. The nation's petroleum reserves are not expected to be exhausted until 2010.

Natural gas reserves are also an important asset with new reserves being discovered both on land and off shore. Gas liquefaction plants and gas pipelines have been constructed. Beginning in 2000, Oman plans to produce and ship some 6.6 million tons of liquefied natural gas annually to Asia.

Omanis hope to convert domestic fuel systems to natural gas in order to release more petroleum for export. Oman has entered into a contract for a ten-year supply of natural gas to the world's first floating methanol plant.

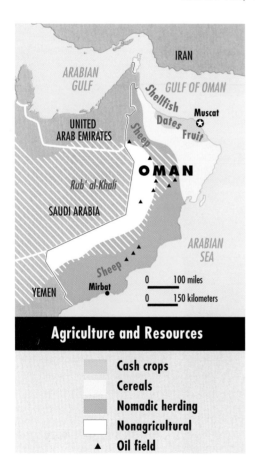

**Agriculture and Resources**

- Cash crops
- Cereals
- Nomadic herding
- Nonagricultural
- ▲ Oil field

The first petroleum refinery in the country began production in 1982. It is hoped that the refinery can meet Oman's domestic need for oil so that imports of refined products can be further reduced.

**A farm in Salalah**

### Improving Agriculture and Fisheries

As oil grew in importance, the income from agriculture, including fishing, has decreased proportionately. Still, 58 percent of the working population is engaged in agriculture, although little land is under cultivation. Current figures show that 4.7 percent of the nation's land is in meadows and pastures, 0.3 percent is used for agriculture, and 95 percent

A scientist at the Marine Research Center studies fish tissue samples.

Date palms account for about half the agricultural area under cultivation.

is made up of desert land and developed areas. Omani economic development plans call for an increase in agricultural production with modernization of farming methods and irrigation projects.

Some 2,500 government-owned research and experimental farms have been established. The government has a ten-year plan for the development of agriculture and fishing.

Water is a major factor in agriculture in this part of the world. In Oman's interior, a system of underground water channels taps the water table. In the main agricultural area along the Batina coast, irrigation systems pump water from wells. Rural power and water networks are to be expanded, and new dams have been built. Efforts are made to conserve floodwater that would otherwise flow along the wadis into the sea. Surveys of underground water are being made with the hope of discovering new water resources.

Farmers at a small, rural vegetable market in Nakal

Dates account for about half of the area being cultivated. Other crops include vegetables, melons, bananas, mangoes, onions, potatoes, papayas, tobacco leaf, and wheat. Farms supply Omanis with almost all their tomatoes, cucumbers, onions, and peppers. Greenhouse production of vegetables began in 1984.

Frankincense is still produced around Dhofar. Imports of this product from other countries have been prohibited to protect local suppliers. Imports of cereals, however, are increasing. A special bank providing loans to farmers and fisherman helps stop the movement of people from rural areas to the cities.

**A Dhofar dairy farmer feeding his cows**

Livestock is raised in Dhofar, where rainfall is more plentiful. Cattle are found in the hills north of Salalah, and goats in the Hajar mountains. While the government has plans for the development of livestock, concern about the environment in Dhofar has led to laws aimed at the reduction of the cows there. Livestock in the country includes cattle, sheep, goats, camels, and chickens.

Fishing has been traditional for the Omanis. In 1980, the Oman National Fisheries Company was organized to grant fishing territories and operate government trawlers and land facilities, such as the processing and freezing plant at Matrah.

The inshore waters provide rock cod, snapper, cuttlefish, and some shellfish—the main source of protein for many Omanis. These fish are also exported and sometimes fed to livestock in Dhofar. Small fishers have been provided with boats and outboard motors. However, many Omanis do not want to change from the subsistence to the commercial level of fishing.

Fishers returning to the isolated village of Kumzar at dusk

Before the coming of oil wealth, the main industry in Oman was involved with traditional handicrafts like silversmithing, weaving, and boat-building. Because Oman's revenues from oil are less than those of some neighboring countries and because of a shortage of labor, it is not likely that the country can develop heavy industry and manufacturing on a large scale.

As the government began to develop the country with roads and buildings after 1970, there was a boom in the construction industry. However, new projects are sometimes tied to oil prices. In a good year, a university can be built. In a bad year, the projects are cut. A large cement factory was completed at Rusail in 1983.

The government is encouraging building in rural areas, especially on social projects and roads. Also, the government is giving private investors cheap land and power, duty exemptions, and low-interest loans to develop small-scale industries. Production of animal feed; the conversion of waste products to fertilizer; and the manufacture of construction materials, paper products, spark plugs, detergents, and perfumes are among the new enterprises.

Although the government wants to develop new industry, it has to consider its labor limitations. A significant number of Indian and Pakistani workers have been involved in the construction and industrial companies. The government has adopted a policy of "Omanizing" the labor force—decreasing its dependence on foreign workers and giving opportunities to the expanding Omani population. New training opportunities are being offered to Omanis.

*Opposite:* **A foreign worker displays fish at the market.**

A copper smelter

## Natural Resources

Geological surveys are being made to locate other mineral deposits. Reserves of copper and chromium ore are being developed with the help of foreign countries and foreign investment. Gold, silver, chromium, gypsum, salt, limestone, iron ore, and marble are mined.

## Water and Power

The industrial changes have led to an increase in water and power needs. Power station expansions have been planned, and rural electrification programs have been started.

## Communication and Transportation Systems

Communication and transportation systems are very important to Oman because of the country's location. Seaports, airports, and roads have all been upgraded and have received foreign funding. Rural air services have been expanded. The Omanis, once great sailors, have developed an intense interest in air travel.

In 1970, the country had no radio station, and no movies were allowed in Oman. Now there are radio stations, color TV, and satellite stations that provide telephone and audiovisual links with the rest of the world. The 1.5 million TV sets mean that there is one set for every 1.4 persons. The print media is represented by three Arabic- and two English-language newspapers and fourteen magazines.

### What Oman Grows, Makes, and Mines

**Agriculture (1996)**

| | |
|---|---|
| Vegetables and melons | 167,000 metric tons |
| Dates | 133,000 metric tons |
| Bananas | 26,000 metric tons |

**Manufacturing (1993; in Omani rials)**

| | |
|---|---|
| Textiles and apparel | 78,290,000 |
| Food products and beverages | 72,930,000 |
| Chemical products | 40,950,000 |

**Mining (1994)**

| | |
|---|---|
| Copper | 6,500 metric tons |
| Silver | 7,275 pounds (3,300 kg) |
| Gold | 165 pounds (75 kg) |

## Tourism and the National Economy

The beauty and mystery of Oman draw tourists to the country. At one time, tourism was not encouraged because of fear that national customs, such as religious observances, dress, and food, would be destroyed. However, Oman is now open but expensive. Visitors spent some U.S.$218 million in Oman in 1994. With 344,000 persons arriving in Oman in 1993, the nation experienced a 79 percent increase in numbers of visitors over the previous year. The country boasts a luxury hotel that is ranked among the best throughout the world.

## Omani Currency and Coins

Many ancient coins from various civilizations have been found in Oman. The first coins minted in Oman were produced in A.D. 708 by a local governor appointed by the Damascus caliph. Today, the national emblem of crossed swords and curved dagger appears on all denominations of currency and coins. A portrait of Sultan Qaboos appears on paper currency.

The monetary unit of Oman is the Omani rial (RO). The rial is divided into 1,000 baisas. Notes are available in values of RO 50, 20, 10, 5, and 1, as well as 500, 250, 200, and 100 baisas. Coins are available in 50 and 25 baisas, which are silver, and 10 and 5 baisas, which are copper. In 1999, one rial was equal to U.S.$2.60.

**Oman International Bank in Nizwa**

New guidebooks help travelers plan for a visit to Oman. Besides sightseeing in the country, tourists can go camel-trekking in the dunes, rock-climbing in the Musandam Peninsula, skin-diving and deep-sea fishing in the Indian Ocean, cave-exploring in the Hajar mountains, and bird-watching in the Dhofar salt marshes.

## Financial Services

Although the banking industry of Oman is smaller than the elaborate systems of some other Gulf states, Oman has both domestic and foreign banks. The government has encouraged employment of Omanis as a higher percentage of bank workers. In 1990, the first Omani stock exchange was opened in Muscat, dealing in shares of local companies.

The Central Bank of Oman and several government development banks deal with government policy. Oman has had government deficits since 1981, and the World Bank has warned that the current spending cannot be sustained. The Omani minister has announced plans for a balanced budget by the year 2000. Foreign investments will be encouraged, and some industry will be shifted to private ownership.

**Weights and Measures**

The metric system is used throughout Oman. Temperatures are measured in the Celsius scale.

# The Omanis

Oman has a richly varied population. Its ancient civilization has allowed time for the introduction of many different kinds of people. Also, the country is situated on trade routes that have brought many new people to the land. The mountains and deserts that carve up the land into compartments help to isolate different groups. Finally, Oman's strong family and tribal relationships help to preserve local customs and traditions.

THERE ARE SIX MAJOR GROUPS OF OMANIS. First are the coastal people who live traditionally by seafaring, trading, and fishing. They include the residents of Muscat, Matrah, Sohar, and Sur. Second, in the north are the people of the Batina coast. These farmers cultivate their crops with water drawn from wells. Third, in the interior, are the people of the Hadhr region. They live in towns like Nizwa and Rustaq and in villages, and depend on water channels to irrigate their crops. Fourth are the Bedouin. They are nomads who live in the plains to the south and the west. Fifth, the Shihuh are a mountain people. They live on the Musandam Peninsula. Sixth are the people of the Dhofar, to the south. They are related in background and language to the people of South Arabia and parts of east Africa.

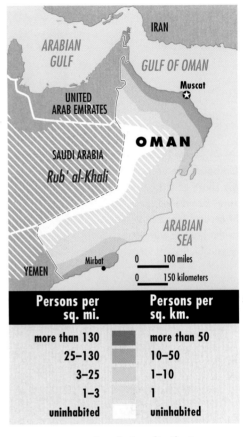

| Persons per sq. mi. | | Persons per sq. km. | |
|---|---|---|---|
| more than 130 | | more than 50 | |
| 25–130 | | 10–50 | |
| 3–25 | | 1–10 | |
| 1–3 | | 1 | |
| uninhabited | | uninhabited | |

**Population distribution in Oman**

## Characteristics of the Coastal People

For many years, Muscat was the chief port for all of Arabia. From December to February, ships sailed to Zanzibar on the northeast monsoon winds. They carried dates to trade for ivory, beeswax, tortoiseshell, and slaves. They sailed home when the wind shifted to the southwesterly monsoon from April to September.

*Opposite:* **Suburban civil servants of Muscat**

Outboard motorboats on the shore of Sidab, a small fishing village east of Muscat. The boats return to the harbor with tuna at sunset.

A receptionist at the Muscat Technical Industrial College

Eventually, the sultans of Oman and Zanzibar cooperated with the British to put down the slave trade. At least, the treatment of the slaves who reached Oman is said to have been less harsh than it was in the Americas and West Indies. According to one report in 1817, the slaves were entitled to a share in the property when the master died.

Even today, people of different national origins and dress mingle in the markets of Muscat and Matrah. Women in bright clothing or dark robes shop in the cloth and jewelry stores. Prices usually are fixed, and bargaining is polite and not as lengthy as in some Near Eastern markets.

Muscat, the capital of Oman, has three different kinds of architecture—traditional Arab, Portuguese, and modern. While much of the old has been cleared away for new buildings, some of the finest old buildings are being preserved. Many modern buildings, such as the palace of the sultan, have incorporated traditional architectural styles.

The merchants of Muscat and Matrah have built fine houses, but most also own a country area where they can escape the heat of the summer. Here, they and their families enjoy the flowers and the plentiful water.

## The People of Oman

Approximately 90 percent of Oman's people are Arabs. The rest of the population includes East Africans, Indians, Iranians, and Pakistanis.

A *falaj* irrigation canal

**Estimated Populations of Key Cities in Oman**

Nizwa : 62,880 (1990)

Muscat: 51,969 (1993)

Matrah: 20,000 (1992)

Salalah: 10,000 (1992)

Nizwa is shown in the photo at right.

## People of the Batina Coast

Along the Batina coast, fishing is an important industry. Fish is important in the diet of the local people and is sold to people in the interior. Many traditional fishing methods are still used, but canoes made of hollowed-out trunks are now fitted with outboard motors. Some dried fish and sharksfin can be exported.

Batina also has many date plantations. Most of the water supply comes from wells operated by pumps. Traces of the ancient canals still exist. In the past, the buckets of well water would be raised with the aid of animals such as a bull, donkey, or camel, walking down an incline. In addition to the dates, almonds and figs are grown in the gardens.

Batina is the main agricultural area. Here the government is exploring the underground water table. A plain between the cultivated area and the mountains provides grazing for camels, goats, and donkeys.

The people of the Batina area along the coast have inter-married with newcomers brought by the sea. Settlers have arrived from India and Africa over the centuries. The Batina women wear thin head-veils that billow out behind them. Purple and black are popular colors here.

## Life in the Interior

The interior lies along the great central mountain range of the Jabal Akhdar or "Green Mountain" as it is sometimes called. Some of its main towns, Nizwa, Rustaq, Iki, and Bahla, were once capitals of the country. The Ibadhi group of Muslims control this area. Outside of Oman, only northwest Africa claims adherents to this division of Islam.

The markets of the interior include many small shops. The silversmiths, with blowlamps and work space in the back of

A rugmaker operates his loom in Wadi Ghul, a center of traditional weaving.

their shops, display decorated guns, jewelry, and other items of their trade out front. Shops for pots and pans feature the traditional work of the coppersmith along with imported items of aluminum and enamel. The gunsmith works on equipment that would be considered antique in markets elsewhere. Spice shops display their wares with the aroma from their products providing an advance advertising as the shopper approaches. Shops that sell fish can be easily identified too. Fish are trucked in now—an advantage over the days when they were brought by camel.

Bookkeepers at the Nizwa livestock auction record every sale in their books.

Shops also sell local products—cloth, pottery, and a sweet called *halwa*. Brown sugar, oranges, limes, dates, bananas, apricots, peaches, mangoes, pomegranates, grapes, wheat, and tobacco are grown in the interior. Alfalfa, which is used to feed livestock, is available in the market.

Animal auctions provide a market for cattle, goats, and sheep. The animals are driven around the ring of buyers as the auctioneer calls out the bids.

Agriculture is the major activity in this region. At one time an even larger part of the land was under cultivation. Many varieties of date palm are grown here.

Water for crop irrigation is obtained by tapping the water table and then leading the water onto the land through water channels. These channels, called *aflaj* (singular, *falaj*), are the main source of irrigation water in Oman. The falaj system was introduced in ancient times by the Persians, and many of the aflaj in use today are over a thousand years old. There are two main types of aflaj in Oman. The first is made up of tunnels that originate at a water source deep under the ground, and the second is composed of surface channels, which typically collect water from wadis after continuous rainfall. Traditional wells are also used for irrigation.

The markets in this area are very much alike. The shops are built of mud brick covered with rough mud mortar. They are usually square and often stand on platforms in rows along narrow streets. The market area is behind walls that can be shut and guarded at night. Some markets are completely covered.

A dried-fish merchant with a buyer at Nizwa souk

Traditional roles exist for men, women, and children in the towns. Men take care of business, attend the mosque, supervise or work in the date plantations or the fields, do the shopping, and take care of the animals. Younger men who are in the armed forces or who are working for wages may be away from their villages for most of the week. Women cook and make coffee or tea for the family and visitors, get the water, prepare the *laban* (yogurt), sew, do the washing, weave, and in some areas do embroidery. Women and small children herd

Two young brothers from Nakal in traditional dress

Women from the interior region in brightly colored garb

the goats, sheep, and poultry. Boys stay with their mother until they are about eight years old. Among the Bedouin, the division of labor may be slightly different, with the men herding the animals and making the coffee.

People in mountain areas tend to wear traditional dress. The men wear white robes, with their silver khanjar, or curved daggers, in their belts. They may carry their rifles with them on holidays to shoot off during the celebration. They wear bright orange, red, or purple cashmere shawls on their heads, draped to give the appearance of a turban.

Women and girls dress in bright colors, such as orange, yellow, or green, and their clothes are edged with silver thread and embroidery. Their heads are covered but not veiled. They may wear an outer garment called a *laisu* that consists of two large pieces of cotton sewn together.

## The Bedouin

The deserts to the west and south of Muscat are home to the Bedouin. These people make up a small minority of the Omani population. More and more of them are moving to permanent housing today. Some settle on the edges of cultivated areas. Some live in tents or in summer houses of mud or palm fronds. Several tribes tend gardens of date palms during the summer.

Bedouin tents vary in size. Some are large and commodious, while others are just big enough for shelter. They are made of woven camel or goat hair. Alternate red and black stripes is typical of western Oman. Women also weave the fabric for rugs and for the trappings of the camels and horses.

Family history is important to the tribes. The Omanis claim descent from the Qahtan tribes of south Arabia and the Nizar of the north. Life is simple and hard. Many of the Bedouin are being drawn to employment in the oil fields of the area.

Many observers have praised the Bedouin for their loyalty, courage, and hospitality. Members of the tribe live with physical hardship—extremes of heat and cold, little water, sandstorms, and sun glare. They carry few possessions with them.

A tribe on the move arises at dawn to awaken their noisy camels. At the call to prayer, the men pray singly or in rows, always facing Mecca as Muslims are required to do. Coffee and bread are made. Even in the desert, coffee is served in a formal manner. One person pours the drops in the small cups, bowing as he hands them to others.

**The women and children of an Oman Bedouin encampment**

The Omani ride their camels in a different manner than most of the Arabs. Either they sit a little behind the hump with a leg on either side of the hump, or else they kneel sitting on the soles of their feet. They like the kneeling position if they are going to gallop. Then it is purely a matter of balance to stay on.

In the desert, the Bedouin are talkative as they ride together. If they meet a stranger, the greetings are formal before news is sought. The hospitality of these desert dwellers has often saved lives.

## The Shihuh

The Shihuh people live in the mountains of the Musandam Peninsula—the northern tip of Oman that is separated from the rest of the country. Although their numbers are small, they are of special interest because many believe that they represent the original people of southern Arabia who were

Supplies are sometimes delivered by helicopter to the isolated Shihuh tribe in the mountains of the Musandam peninsula.

driven into the mountains where they stayed for protection. Members of this tribe carry a small ax of a special shape.

The Shihuh live in mud or stone dwellings. Some have homes on barren hillsides where the rainwater is stored in tanks. They grow patches of wheat or barley. Those who live on the coast fish and, in the past, dove for pearls.

One group of the Shihuh speak a language that is similar to Persian. Their center is the town of Kumzar, which is high in the rocks with little flat land around it. They bury their dead under the family houses—a tradition that is also practiced in some other parts of the Middle East.

## People of Dhofar

The Dhofaris live in the extreme southern part of Oman, separated from the north by some 600 miles (966 km) of desert. Dhofar was a primary producer of frankincense and had close trade relations with the people of Yemen. However, Dhofar has been linked with northern Oman for more than 100 years. Since Sultan Qaboos bin Said is half Dhofari, there is a special family relationship now.

The Dhofaris live in the mountains and on the plains. The mountain people are divided into several classes. The Qara were traditionally the masters and the Shhero were the serfs. Then there are the Arabas of al-Kathir, and in the lower valleys, the Mahra. All these people depend on coastal cities for trade and supplies.

The mountain people are also dependent on their animals. They put the animals to pasture on grass that grows well following the monsoon. Dhofar gets more rainfall than some other parts of Oman. The people of the various tribes speak a variety of languages as well as Arabic dialects.

Salalah is the capital of Dhofar and the home of many people who came from Africa. The African influence can be seen in the rhythms of the holiday dances and the bright colors the women love to wear.

## Life on the Islands

Oman owns two groups of islands—Masirah to the north and the Kuria Muria Islands in the south. Until the reign of Sultan Qaboos, the residents of Masirah Island were not allowed to put up any permanent buildings. This restriction was their punishment for the massacre of a ship's crew in 1904. They used to live in palm frond dwellings or build shelters out of oil drums discarded from the British air base there.

Oman gave the Kuria Muria Islands—a group of five islands off the coast of Dhofar—to the British in 1854. In return, the British foreign secretary sent a gift of a snuffbox. At first, a British company went into the business of collecting guano—bird droppings used for fertilizer. However, the license to this business was terminated when the company did not make its required payments to the government. The British returned the islands to Oman in 1967. Today, a small number of fishers live there.

## Omani Names

Usually, Omanis are addressed by their first names after introductions. So "Mr. Muhammad" would refer to his friend as "Mr. Abdullah," and foreign visitors would be "Mr. Michael" or "Ms. Susan," for example. In print, Mr. Abdullah would be referred to by his full name, for instance Abdullah bin Ali bin Salem (Abdullah, whose father is Ali, and whose grandfather is Salem). The name of the tribe is sometimes added too. Why so elaborate? Omanis use only about fifty names, all of which are closely associated with the Islamic religion. So this elaborate naming system is needed to tell one Abdullah from another.

**Road signs in Arabic and English**

## Languages

Oman's official language is Arabic, although English is also used in business. One unusual feature of Oman is the number of languages spoken by its residents, sometimes instead of—or in addition to—Arabic. Some of these languages are related to the ancient south Arabian languages that predated Arabic. Inscriptions in this ancient language have been found as far away as Greece and Ethiopia. The unusual characteristics of these languages may indicate that the Omani culture stretched way back in time.

Arabic is greatly honored since it is the language of the Koran, the holy book of Islam. Arabic can be written in a very elaborate way that has become an art form. However, more cursive forms are used in everyday work. The alphabet is complicated. Each letter has four forms depending on its position—whether it is standing alone or is at the beginning, middle, or end of a word. There are no capital letters. As for the spoken Arabic, no "p" sound exists because it becomes a "b." Even more of a problem for foreigners are the sounds in Arabic that have no counterpart in English.

### Everyday Omani phrases

| Arabic in Roman characters | English |
| --- | --- |
| Sa-laam Al-ay-kum | Peace be unto you. (Usual greeting) |
| Wah-lay kum sa-laam | And upon you, peace. (Usual response) |
| Ma-harbah | Hello |
| Kaif Halik? | How are you? (Said to a man) |
| Kaif Halish? | How are you? (Said to a woman) |
| In-shal-lah | If God wills it |

# Ibadhi Muslims

Oman is an unusual Arab country because people of religions other than Islam are present in significant numbers. In addition, most of the Muslims are Ibadhis rather than Sunnis or Shiites. According to 1994 estimates, about 28 percent of the people are Hindus—a reflection of Oman's close trade relations over the centuries with India and the Spice Islands, as well as the number of foreign workers employed in Oman today.

ABOUT 14.7 PERCENT OF THE POPULATION ARE Christians. Christianity in pre-Islamic times was associated with traditions about the mission of St. Thomas, one of the disciples of Jesus. However, the Christian communities died out by the ninth century. The Portuguese brought Christianity back, but they were driven out in the 1600s. In the twentieth century, Christian missionaries established medical and educational institutions.

The majority of the population—estimated at 53.5 percent according to the 1994 census—are Muslims. Approximately 75 percent are Ibadhi Muslims while 25 percent are Sunnis. Some Shiites are found in the merchant classes. In most Arab countries, Sunnis are in the majority, followed by Shiites.

Opposite: **The ruins of a _kibla_, or altar, which Muslims face when they pray**

## Muslim Beliefs

The five duties of a Muslim are (1) to say and accept the statement: "There is no god but God and Muhammad is his Prophet," (2) to pray five times daily, (3) to give alms, (4) to keep the fast of not eating or drinking between sunrise and sunset during the month of Ramadan, and (5) if possible, to make a

### Religious Life in Oman

Most Omanis are Muslims. About 75 percent of Omani Muslims practice Ibadhi Islam, a strict form of that religion. The rest practice Sunni Islam or Shia Islam. Other religions practiced in Oman are Hinduism and Christianity.

pilgrimage or *hajj* to Mecca at least once during a lifetime. Mecca is a holy city associated with the life of Muhammad and is now in Saudi Arabia.

The first pillar, the *Shahadah*, is a confession of faith that the Muslim must declare as belief. Of course, there is more to

**A new mosque given to the people of Rustaq by Sultan Qaboos**

Islamic beliefs—Paradise, angels, the Last Day. The Shahadah, however, is repeated many times during the day.

*Salat*, or ritual prayer is required five times a day, at dawn, noon, late afternoon, sunset, and after sunset. The believer prepares by a ritual washing—water if available, but sand will do where there is no water. The prayer begins in a standing position and follows with bows and prostration until the forehead touches the ground. Quotations from the Koran or other sources are repeated silently. The Koran is the holy book of the Muslims, containing the revelations given to Muhammad.

*Zakat* is the giving of alms to the needy. It is based on a formula depending on the kinds of property owned by the believer. In addition, contributions above what is required are seen as a way of gaining merit.

*Sawn* is the fast during Ramadan—a month that depends on a lunar calendar so it changes throughout the secular year. Muslims fast for the entire day, from daybreak until sundown. Food, drink, and smoking are forbidden during this period. The family shares a meal before dawn and after sunset. When the month of Ramadan falls during the long and hot days of summer, the fasting can be a real test of self-control. Travelers, the sick, and some women are excepted from this requirement.

Finally, the *hajj*, or pilgrimage to Mecca, is expected of Muslims at least once during their lifetime, if they can afford the trip. Some make the trip repeatedly, but for others it takes years of preparation. The ceremonies in Mecca take several days and involve circling the Kaaba and kissing the black stone in one of its corners.

**A small mosque in the interior of Oman**

The *shariah*, or the Law, is the statement of the total way of life Muslims are commanded to live. Different groups within Islam have different views of the shariah.

Muslims can pray individually or worship together in a building called a mosque. This mosque often has a tower called a minaret from which the faithful are called to prayer. In the past, a man would climb the tower to make the call. Today, tape recordings are often used.

Muslims do not have priests that function as a go-between God and humans. Religious leaders or teachers are called imams. At the Friday service at the mosque, a teacher may lead the worshippers. Friday is the Sabbath observed by the Muslims. The term *Islam* means "surrender to the will of God."

## Ibadhi Islam Comes to Oman

Unlike many of the Muslim countries, Oman was not conquered by the military force of the followers of Muhammad. The tribal council of the Azd tribe accepted Islam, and most of the Arab population followed—although not without some tests and trials.

The Azd tribe was an important force in Basra, a center of Muslim influence in what is now southern Iraq. This tribe was instrumental in bringing the form of Islam known as Ibadhism to Oman.

The Ibadhis wanted to restore the country to what it had been during the life of Muhammad and when the first caliphs were in power. The Ibadhis believed that later caliphs had corrupted the teaching. They believed that the position of caliph should not necessarily go to a member of the prophet's family, but should be given to the man best able to lead. In this view, they were closer to the Sunnis than the Shiites. Today, Muslims in many countries follow leaders called imams.

Also, unlike the Sunnis and the Shiites, the Ibadhis do not believe that there needs to be a permanent and visible leader. When appropriate, a leader should be elected, but in times of

Muslims are called to worship from a minaret.

**Religious Holidays**

Because the Islamic calendar year is shorter than the Gregorian calendar year used in the United States and Canada, specific dates for Islamic holidays vary. The most important religious holidays in Oman are:

**Islamic New Year**
**The Prophet's Birthday**
**Ascension of the Prophet**
**Ramadan**
**Eid al-Fitr**
**Eid al-Adha**

## The True Religion

The Omani historian as-Salimi said: "The true religion has been compared to a bird: its egg was laid in Medina [where Muhammad lived], it hatched in Basra and flew to Oman."

persecution, it may be appropriate for Muslims to conceal their actual beliefs. There can be more than one imam to serve different areas.

The Ibadhis claim that their beliefs are a century or so older than those of other Muslims. Their way of worship is plain and simple. They do not use music. Their mosques tend to be of a simpler style without much decoration. Generally, they have

The burial tomb of an important Ibadhi imam

been moderate and tolerant in their treatment of others though they themselves have been persecuted by other Islamic groups. Nevertheless, the Ibadhi imams are very powerful in the interior of Oman, and have often been a force against the sultans' efforts to modernize the country.

## Other Islamic Groups in Oman

People in the central part of Oman have tended to adhere to the Ibadhi form of Islam. The Sunnis and Shiites live along the coasts. Some of the tribes follow the Sunni views. One tribe has adopted Wahhabism, a very strict interpretation of Islam that came from Saudi Arabia. The Shiites count some adherents among the merchant class.

The ruins of Dariyah, where the Wahhabi Islamic movement gained strength

### Omani Religious Leaders

Abdullah bin Ibadh al-Murri al-Tamimi, a teacher in Basra in the seventh century, urged a return to a pure form of Islam. He was dissatisfied with some of the corruption that he believed had been accepted by Muslims since the death of the prophet Muhammad. He reacted against some of the harsh persecution practiced by other reforming groups. Instead of killing Muslims who did not accept a particular version of Islam, Abdullah discouraged the use of force against people who did not agree. He gave his name to the movement that was to take hold in Oman.

An Omani merchant colleague of Abdullah bin Ibadh named Abu Shaatha Jabir bin Zayd was responsible for the spread of these teachings to Oman. When the Ibadhis were persecuted by the Sunni caliphs and the Wahhabi tribes, they went underground with secret meetings until they were free of persecution. Their isolation in the mountains of Oman helped their survival.

# Omani Culture

Although Oman has undergone great changes since 1970 when the present sultan took over the government, Sultan Qaboos has tried to preserve the best of the traditional culture. Evidence of his success can be found in the family, the arts, and even in sports.

## Family Life and Customs

FAMILY CAN BE VERY IMPORTANT TO SURVIVAL IN A COUNTRY where the environment is not always kind to humans. Tribes made up of extended families have played an important role in Oman's history. Islam has reinforced the importance of the family through its laws on marriage and divorce.

Because the family relationship is so important, so are marriage arrangements. Under the law of Islam, it is possible for a man to have four wives, but the man is supposed to treat all wives equally. Usually, only the rich can afford to support more than one wife, and even then there are complications about equal treatment. Most marriages in Oman involve one wife and one husband.

To obtain a divorce, a husband must say three times to his wife: "I divorce you." A woman can petition a judge for divorce on grounds of non-support, adultery, or impotency. However, divorce is unusual and may not be as easy as it sounds because of the financial responsibilities and the need for the care of the children. If a woman is divorced, she returns to her own family and takes her children under the age of five. The father usually takes the older children to his family.

*Opposite:* **Children entertain themselves at a playground in Alayjah, a section of Sur. Sur is Oman's shipbuilding center.**

**A young Omani girl, who in the past could be eligible for marriage at age eleven or twelve**

## Wedding Customs

In the past it was customary for a girl to be engaged and married at the age of eleven or twelve. These marriages were arranged by the families involved. The preferred match was a man marrying his first cousin by his father's brother. If husband and wife came from the same village, they may have seen each other. However, if the bride came from another town, the two might never have met.

Traditionally, when this marriage is the first for the girl, the negotiations are carried on between the relatives, but the girl must give her consent to the arrangement. A bride price, called *mahr*, had to be paid for a valid marriage. Though the amount varied in different parts of the country, it could be quite high. Now, some of these customs are changing. Sultan Qaboos set a fixed bride price throughout the country.

The mahr becomes the property of the wife and remains with her even if she is divorced. While the bride price may be paid in money, usually some part is in gifts of various types, such as jewelry, which may be displayed around the reception room at the wedding celebration.

After the negotiations and signing of the legal contract and the oral acceptance in front of a religious judge, the wedding celebration begins. Men and women have separate parties with feasting, dancing, and, in some places, singing.

The bride—especially in the interior of the country—may have her hands, feet, and face painted with designs in henna—a yellow paste made from the orange flowers of the shooran shrub. Traditionally, on the first night the bride wears green clothes associated with fertility. The celebrations may go on for several days but end when the newlyweds are escorted to their new home.

Generally, Oman has not placed the same restrictions on the dress and the seclusion of women that are found elsewhere in the Arab world. The return to more conservative dress that is going on in other Arab countries may change the attitudes of Omani women about this custom. Also, the increased opportunity for education and travel may change traditional ways in the future.

Omani women do not dress conservatively.

According to custom, a woman's social status was greatly increased by the birth of a son, though girls were welcomed too. Male circumcision was usually performed at 15 days or six years, although some elaborate ceremonies surrounding this practice have been described for a boy 15 years of age.

When a member of the family dies, the body is washed, sprinkled with spices, and placed in a white muslin shroud. Burial usually takes place the same day as the death unless the person passes away during the night. The male relatives carry the body to the grave, and the wife traditionally goes into a period of mourning for four months and ten days.

**A beautiful geometric design of the Islamic culture**

## Arts in Oman

Because Islam has certain prohibitions about the portrayal of human figures, much of traditional Muslim art centers around beautiful designs of elaborate geometric patterns in decorations. The objection to human figures is based on the command not to make images that can be worshipped.

The metalworkers of Oman have developed this decorative art to a high degree on such items as the traditional dagger—the khanjar—and its sheath, as well as on utensils such as coffee pots, incense burners, rosewater sprinklers, and jewelry. These artists use gold, silver, and copper.

Almost all Omani men wear a khanjar on formal occasions. This curved dagger in its sheath is secured by rings to the belt and worn in front. It is an important emblem on the Omani flag. Men also may have decorated silver gunpowder horns. They may carry silver pipes and have toilet sets that consist of a toothpick and an ear spoon.

Women wear much of their wealth in the form of gold and silver jewelry. Rings, earrings, nose rings, head ornaments, bracelets, armlets, anklets, necklaces, and chains with amulets containing verses from the Koran may be part of a woman's wardrobe. Rings are worn on the feet too. Each ring in the customary five-finger set per hand has a different name. Gold coins are often incorporated in the jewelry—especially in some of the bridal headdresses. Different parts of the country have different designs for jewelry.

Utensils, too, may have different shapes depending on where they are made. Coffee pots are in special demand since an Omani host traditionally offers coffee to anyone who calls on him. The traditional Omani meal of a mound of rice and meat with many kinds of garnishes is usually eaten with the right hand. (The left hand is reserved for bathroom functions.) Water used to rinse the fingers is offered in decorated copper bowls. In wealthy households, rosewater may be

Decorative khanjars (daggers) are worn by Omani men.

The traditional meal served to guests includes roast lamb on a bed of rice, boiled eggs, and fresh fruit.

**A traditional chest decorated with brass**

sprinkled on the hands or head of guests from metal containers. Also incense may be carried to the guests in metal burners. The incense is the signal for departure. All these utensils may have complex decorations.

Traditional chests decorated with brass nails are found in homes and were used by sailors. Silver-decorated guns are popular with collectors.

Pottery from ancient times to the present has been an important craft. Good clay is not available everywhere, but Bahla in northern Oman has a reputation for fine products. Techniques are often passed down through the generations in a family. One potter dated the founding of his business to the sixteenth century.

**A woman weaving in Khabura**

Weaving was a traditional art that began with the carding and spinning of thread from cotton plants. Since little cotton is now grown and cloth is imported, the craft was dying out. Only a few old men still had the skill. Now the government has established centers for women to teach the old crafts. Near Khabura, women produce narrow rugs and animal trappings on traditional looms. Goat hair is used in the weaving at Bahla. Red and black rugs are typical. Ibri and Nizwa have been centers for the prized indigo dye.

Boat-building, an art at which Omanis have excelled for centuries, tended to be the specialty of a few families. Ships ranging from sea-going warships to palm-frond boats have been built in Oman.

A traditional dhow being built in Sur

A carved wooden door of
the Rustaq fort

Woodcarving—especially elaborately carved doors—is a specialty of Oman. The wood comes from east Africa or India. Even simple houses built of mud were likely to have intricately carved wooden doors. Many of the huge ships also carried decorations, but not many of these have survived. We know about them from photographs and drawings.

## Architecture and Fine Arts

Ancient buildings are valued in Oman. More than 500 forts, castles, watchtowers, and fortified walls remain—and some are being restored by the government. The mud-brick fort in Bahla probably dates to pre-Islamic times and has been placed on the UNESCO World Heritage list. Some of the nineteenth-century merchant homes are also being restored. Mosques and souks, or markets, are also of historic interest.

Since 1970, many beautiful modern buildings have been constructed. These concrete and air-conditioned buildings often incorporate traditional features, such as white-washing and arches.

In the early 1980s, the government began to encourage the development of fine arts. Instructors and materials were made available to artists. The government sent students to Egypt and Iraq for further study. At first, artists painted in a naturalistic manner. Later, artists worked with abstract subjects and calligraphy, or designs with words. In 1992, the Omani Society of Fine Arts was founded in Muscat.

### Anwar Khamis Sonia

The artist Anwar Khamis Sonia was born in 1948 and trained in Britain. He painted landscapes and scenes of life. His most famous painting is *Old Door*, 1988.

## Music

Music was not encouraged by the Ibadhi. However, the music for festivals involves drums, a wind instrument made from a horn, a straight pipe, and a stringed instrument known as a *rababa*. These instruments provide a background for both male and female dancing groups. Probably the most famous dance is the sword dance, which is done with swords, daggers, and small round shields.

Sailors have always had their own songs and chants. Some of the Bedouin tribes also have special songs.

## Special Collections

Language has always had special importance in Islamic cultures because of the importance of the Koran, Islam's holy book. Books that were written by hand were decorated with elaborate calligraphy. Unfortunately, many ancient manuscripts were destroyed during the many wars of this country. Some of the material that was taken out of the country in times of conflict is being collected now by the government.

The Ruwi National Museum displays its most important exhibits on the upper floor. The central area of the main hall focuses on silverwork. Then there are examples of typical rooms of houses with a display of traditional clothing. The rear of the main hall shows the trade routes followed by Omani sailors, along with models of different kinds of ships. The treasures of some of the sultans are displayed. The final room is dedicated to space exploration and includes two small Omani flags that U.S. astronauts carried to the moon and back.

**Sadek Abdowani**

Sadek Abdowani is the editor-in-chief of *a-Usra* magazine and a former assistant secretary general of the Shoura Assembly. Educated at Kuwait University, he has worked as a diplomat and is the author of *The Saudi-Gulf Relations, 1740–1820* and various short stories. He has received medals as president of the Volleyball Association and a certificate of thanks from the sultan as a scholar on historical research. He enjoys table tennis and swimming.

## Museums for Every Interest

The Ministry of National Heritage and Culture has established a number of museums. All except one are in the Muscat area. The Oman Museum in Qurm, opened in 1974, contains archaeological items and Islamic manuscripts and artifacts. The National Museum in Ruwi has exhibits relating to Omani crafts and maritime history. The Armed Forces Museum features types of weapons. The Omani-French Museum displays traditional crafts and costumes as well as items related to the relationship of Oman and France. A Children's Museum in Qurm provides hands-on science exhibits. The Natural History Museum specializes in the geography, geology, flora, and fauna of the country. Away from Muscat, the Sohar fort has a museum that features weapons and local handicrafts.

Oman has had its share of scholars especially in religion, history, and genealogy. Modern authors whose work have been valued are Abdulla bin Humaid as-Salimi, Muhammad bin Abdulla as-Salimi, and Salim bin Humud as-Siyabi.

Who do you think is the best-known Omani in fiction? If you guessed Sinbad the Sailor, you are right. The story from *The Thousand and One Nights* (also called *The Arabian Nights*) was one that Scheherazade is supposed to have told to save her life. Sinbad's seven voyages have been the subject of modern cartoons.

Omanis playing their national sport, football (called soccer in the United States and Canada), on a beach in Sur

## Popular Sports

While the national sport is football (known as soccer in the United States and Canada), a wide variety of sports is available, from water sports to equestrian sports and including cricket, volleyball, bowling, and even ice-skating. Oman first entered the Olympic Games in 1984 in Los Angeles, represented by nine shooters and seven track and field

### A Soccer Star

Mohammed Kathiri of Oman was awarded the Golden Ball as the most valuable player in the Under-17 World Soccer Championships. He scored goals with a variety of long-distance and cleverly placed shots. The Omani team achieved fourth place in this 1995 competition, beating Germany and eliminating Nigeria, which had held the cup from the previous year.

athletes. Omani athletes achieved fourth place in the 1995 Under-17 World Soccer competition for young players.

Older boys and men like to play a game of strategy called *How-walis*. It is a little like backgammon—another Arabian game. Small holes in the ground, or cups, each contain two counters, such as beads or stones. The object of the game is to capture the opponent's pieces.

Men playing an Omani board game

### An Omani Role Model

Raya bint Saif al-Riyami runs a travel business and a hang-gliding school. She is a director of Oman's Girl Guides and a past president of Oman's Women's Association. She volunteers to help mothers with handicapped children and holds workshops in health counseling and family planning. She is a role model for women in Oman today.

# A Visit to an Omani Family

The day of any "typical" Omani is going to be very different, depending on the person's way of life. He or she might be hitching up a camel, going fishing, selling or shopping in a souk, weaving, teaching, planning new construction, judging a case, or administering a government agency. The lifestyles of Omanis may also depend on where they live.

So let's pick two schoolchildren—Miriam and Abdullah—the daughter and son of a businessman and his wife who live in Muscat, Oman's capital. We'll follow them through a day. It will be a special day because, after school, they are going to entertain Jane, a young visitor from North America who has accompanied her family on a business trip to Oman. The Omani family is planning to treat their visitors to a traditional Arab meal.

*Opposite:* **A woman from the province of Dhofar**

**Young girls from Kumzar**

Young girls wearing jewelry
for a religious holiday

Miriam and Abdullah feel excited about the day ahead when they hear the first call to prayer and climb out of their beds just before sunrise to begin the day. They face Mecca and worship in the Muslim way. The other four calls to prayer will come at noon, mid-afternoon, sunset, and twilight. If their guests are present then, they may excuse themselves and go to another room for their prayers, or they may take a moment of silent reflection, or they may even skip that prayer.

Miriam and Abdullah eat a light breakfast of fruit and a porridge made from grain. Then they are off to school. Their parents think education is very important for both of them, and the sultan has made education available to all his people.

During school, the two daydream about the party to come. Their father knows Jane's family well, since they have had business dealings with them over the years. They could have taken Jane's family to a fine restaurant with a variety of ethnic foods, but Jane's father wanted his daughter to see what a traditional Arab meal might be like. So they are going to put on a real celebration in their home—even to the point of dressing Jane in some of Miriam's old festival clothes.

Of course, Miriam and Abdullah will have to forgo their usual after-school games with friends. But what stories they will have to tell tomorrow about how their foreign friend liked their entertainment!

After school, Abdullah and Miriam hurry home. Their mother has cleared away the table and chairs from the center of their dining room and put cushions and mats on the floor. She has also laid out party clothes for her children and Jane.

## Games Omani Children Play

*Darwaza* is a game similar to London Bridge Is Falling Down. Two players face each other with arms raised or lowered to trap those passing underneath the arms. In Oman, the players' arms symbolize the Muscat city gate instead of London Bridge.

*Al-Khatum* is a version of hide-and-seek. Skill in picking up jacks or sticks is tested in *Talatha-talatha* (Three-three) or *Khamsa-khamsa* (Five-five).

Older boys play *Al-Rhume*. In this game, the person who is "it" must stay behind a rope while others try to get their caps, which are left within reach, without getting caught.

*Solah* involves hitting a ball and running to a specific place, as in baseball or cricket. Soccer is especially popular with boys, who are always practicing the skills of this game.

When Jane and her family arrive, Miriam takes Jane into her bedroom to help her put on her Omani outfit. Their mothers soon join them. Omani women dress modestly but their outfits are colorful. Women in some Arab countries wear black coveralls in public.

First, Jane puts on a pair of baggy trousers gathered at the ankle with rich embroidery. Then she is helped into a caftan—a loosely fitted garment that falls just below her knees. Miriam's mother produces a face veil and asks Jane how she would like to eat with a veil on. Jane looks to her mother, puzzled at what to say. Miriam's mother laughs and tells Jane that she won't need to try it. She just wanted to show her what some of the Bedouin wear who follow the strict Wahhabi version of Islam.

Jane's outfit is not complete yet. Next comes a *wiqaiah*—a beautiful headdress worn on special occasions. Miriam's mother shows Jane a simpler version called a *lihaff* that is attached at the top of the head and then extends to the back. Finally, Jane is decked out with a colorful shawl and a lot of gold and silver jewelry. She decides against having henna designs painted on her hands—a decoration that would take some time. Shoes are removed before going to the living room.

Jane is led out to show off her outfit to the rest of the family. Abdullah is wearing an ankle-length, white *dish-dasha* covered with a black cloak. The cloak is edged with gold embroidery, worn across the shoulders, and fastened at the neck. He wears a traditional khanjar, or curved dagger in his belt. Next to the khanjar is a small silver container containing kohl—eye shadow to reduce the glare from the desert sun—and tweezers to remove thorns or slivers. Jane's father remarks that American football players also use black cosmetics near their eyes to cut down on glare.

**A thirteen-year-old boy from interior Oman wearing a *kimah* hat**

On his head, Abdullah is wearing a closely fitting skullcap. Over that is a *masser*, a square cloth of cotton with elaborate patterns woven into the material. The masser is carefully folded and wound into a turban. Abdullah's father explains that he can tell which part of Oman a man comes from by his headdress. The black cloak is worn only for very formal occasions, so Abdullah takes it off before he gets down to the serious business of eating.

The families go into the dining room. Because foreign guests are being entertained, the men and women will eat together even though they are not all

## Khawa

*Khawa*—Omani coffee—is a mixture of coffee beans and cardamom, an herb of the ginger family. In the desert, coffee is made over an open fire or brazier, and a touch of rosewater or saffron is added. The small cups in which it is poured only contain about 1 ounce (28 grams).

family members. Jane sits down on a pillow along the side of the room where Miriam suggests that she will be most comfortable. Miriam tells her that while Omanis try not to point their feet at anyone, she should feel free to cross her legs if that is more comfortable for her. Jane's father tells her she should not use her left hand in the dishes put before her. In desert areas, the left hand is used for bathroom functions and is considered unclean.

Miriam's mother pours heavily sugared coffee from a silver pot with a long curved spout. They drink from small cups with no handles. Miriam's mother cautions Jane to try it with the sweet she offers with it because most visitors find the taste

bitter. She keeps refilling the cups until people signal that they do not want more by slightly shaking their cups from side to side or by turning them over.

Next, Jane is given dates to taste. The ripe dates are the sweetest. Abdullah tells Jane that although he likes dates in the many ways that his mother serves them, his favorite is date honey—a syrup used on desserts. Other fruits are set out on a plate.

Then comes a whole series of dishes in which various seasonings are used. Oman's location benefited from the spice trade, but Omani's use seasoning that is delicate rather than spicy. Beef, chicken, and fish dishes are set before them. Pork is not used because the family is Muslim. *Mishkak*, small bits of meat skewered on date palm frond, is also served. The main meal, which is usually served in the mid-afternoon, always includes rice, potatoes, or bread. The trick of eating rice by hand is to clump it into a small ball.

Finally, the desert called *halwah* is served. It is very sweet and, according to Miriam, takes a long time to prepare. It has to be cooked, strained, and then blended until it is thick.

Finally, Abdullah's father passes around a brazier of burning coals on which frankincense is placed. Everyone allows the aroma to surround their clothing and hair. This event signals the end of the evening, and Jane and her family rise from their cushions. Of course, Jane has to return her outfit for the evening and get back into her own things. What a treat she and her family have experienced, enjoying the hospitality of an Omani home!

## A Frisky Goat

Who discovered coffee? According to one account, it was a goat in Yemen. The goatherd noticed that his goat seemed unusually frisky after the animal nibbled the leaves of the coffee plant. Trying the plant himself, he discovered that it helped him to stay awake. At one time, this part of Arabia held a monopoly on the coffee business. Then the drink became very popular in Europe and other countries acquired the plant.

*Opposite:* **A spice shop selling traditional spices for cooking**

Miriam and Abdullah live in a period of tension and transition. Modern education may open windows to new lifestyles that may be in conflict with more traditional ones. Miriam, especially, may see changes in the role of women as more of them are educated and seek public roles rather than being content to work at home.

Unless new natural resources are discovered, the young Omanis of today will have to decide how they can shift their economy to a new basis from one where oil was the chief asset. Abdullah, under the new policy of Omanization of the workforce, may be trained as a leader in new enterprises.

Some of the current movements in Islam may challenge the predominant Ibadhism of Oman. Already, followers of some of the more extreme forms of Islam from Saudi Arabia have tried to encourage more conservative Islamic dress and habits in Oman.

Living in the Middle East with Iraq and Saudi Arabia as near neighbors means that there is the possibility of armed hostilities. The tensions of this area make diplomatic efforts both important and difficult. The Gulf War in 1991 between the United Nations forces and Iraq after Iraq invaded Kuwait

clearly showed the problems facing small countries in the Middle East.

The future may not be easy for young Omanis. But the courage and enterprise that Oman has shown in the past will surely provide a good basis for living in the future. Omanis, with their pride in the past and the great gains they have made in recent years, have given Miriam and Abdullah a sound heritage on which they will build the future.

**A platter and cushions prepared for serving a traditional meal**

# Timeline

| Omani History | | World History | |
|---|---|---|---|
| | | **2500** B.C. | Egyptians build the Pyramids and Sphinx in Giza. |
| Migration of Arab clans to Oman. | **9th century** B.C. | | |
| | | 563 B.C. | Buddha is born in India. |
| North Oman comes under Persian control. | **4th century** B.C.— A.D. **800** | | |
| | | A.D. **313** | The Roman emperor Constantine recognizes Christianity. |
| Oman and the entire Arabian Peninsula convert to Islam. | A.D. **630** | 610 | The prophet Muhammad begins preaching a new religion called Islam. |
| Julanda bin Masud is elected imam; Oman continues under imam rule until 1154. | 751 | | |
| | | 1054 | The Eastern (Orthodox) and Western (Roman) Churches break apart. |
| | | 1066 | William the Conqueror defeats the English in the Battle of Hastings. |
| | | 1095 | Pope Urban II proclaims the First Crusade. |
| Banu Nabhan dynasty is established. | 1151 | 1215 | King John seals the Magna Carta. |
| | | 1300s | The Renaissance begins in Italy. |
| | | 1347 | The Black Death sweeps through Europe. |
| Dynastic rule is challenged by the imams. | 1428 | 1453 | Ottoman Turks capture Constantinople, conquering the Byzantine Empire. |
| | | 1492 | Columbus arrives in North America. |
| | | 1500s | The Reformation leads to the birth of Protestantism. |
| Coastal area, including the port city of Muscat, falls under Portuguese control. | 1507 | | |
| Portuguese are driven out by Sultan bin Saif. | 1650 | | |

## Omani History

| | |
|---|---|
| Civil war between the Hinawis and the Ghafiris. | **Early 18th century** |
| Independent Sultanate of Muscat and Oman established by Ahmad bin Said, founder of the Al Bu Said dynasty that still rules Oman. | **1749** |
| Muscat and Oman becomes the most powerful state in Arabia, ruling Zanzibar until 1861. | **19th century** |
| The Sultanate of Muscat and Oman gains independence from Britain; Treaty of Friendship is signed. | **1951** |
| Oil is discovered. | **1964** |
| Sultan Said bin Taimur is replaced by his son Qaboos bin Said in a bloodless coup. | **1970** |
| Left-wing rebels in Dhofar, who had been supported by South Yemen, are defeated with military assistance from the United Kingdom, ending a 10-year revolution. | **1975** |
| Consultative Council is set up; Oman helps establish the six-member Gulf Cooperation Council. | **1981** |
| Oman joins the United States–led coalition to oppose Iraq's occupation of Kuwait. | **1991** |
| Women are allowed to be members of the Consultative Council. | **1994** |

## World History

| | |
|---|---|
| **1776** | The Declaration of Independence is signed. |
| **1789** | The French Revolution begins. |
| **1865** | The American Civil War ends. |
| **1914** | World War I breaks out. |
| **1917** | The Bolshevik Revolution brings Communism to Russia. |
| **1929** | Worldwide economic depression begins. |
| **1939** | World War II begins, following the German invasion of Poland. |
| **1957** | The Vietnam War starts. |
| **1989** | The Berlin Wall is torn down as Communism crumbles in Eastern Europe. |
| **1996** | Bill Clinton re-elected U.S. president. |

# Fast Facts

**Official name:** Sultanat Uman (Sultanate of Oman)

**Capital:** Muscat

Sohar

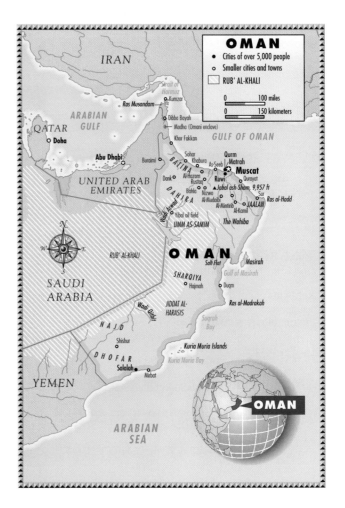

A souk in Salalah

The Omani flag

Sultan Qaboos

| | |
|---:|:---|
| **Official language:** | Arabic |
| **Major religion:** | Ibadhi Islam |
| **Founding date:** | 1749 |
| **Founder:** | Ahmad bin Said |
| **National anthem:** | "Nashid as-Salaam as Sultani" ("Sultan's National Anthem") |
| **Government:** | Constitutional monarchy |
| **Chief of state:** | Sultan |
| **Head of government:** | Sultan |
| **Area:** | 119,507 square miles (309,500 sq km) |
| **Dimensions:** | North–south, 500 miles (805 km) East–west, 400 miles (644 km) |
| **Coordinates of geographic center:** | 21° 00' N, 57° 00' E |
| **Borders:** | Bounded on the north by the Gulf of Oman, on the east and south by the Arabian Sea, on the southwest by Yemen, on the west by Saudi Arabia, and on the northwest by Saudi Arabia and the United Arab Emirates. |
| **Highest elevation:** | Jabal ash-Sham, 9,957 feet (3,035 m) |
| **Lowest elevation:** | Sea level |
| **Climate:** | Desert climate, which varies from region to region. The coastal areas are hot and humid with temperatures reaching as high as 116°F (47°C). The interior is hot and dry. In the mountainous regions, the climate is temperate. |

Holiday attire

A Portuguese fort, Muscat

Currency

**Average anuual precipitation:** 1.5–3.5 inches (4–9 centimeters) except in the Dhofar Region, which receives up to 25 inches (63.5 centimeters).

**National population (1996 est.):** 2,265,000 (est. 1998)

**Population of largest cities:**

| | |
|---|---|
| Nizwa | 62,880 |
| Muscat | 51,969 |
| Matrah | 20,000 |
| Salalah | 10,000 |

**Famous landmarks:**
- ▶ ***Al-Alam Palace.*** Muscat (royal palace of the sultan)
- ▶ ***Fort Jalali*** and ***Fort Mirani.*** Muscat (forts built by the Portuguese)
- ▶ ***Omani-French Museum.*** Muscat (holds cultural artifacts and diplomatic documents from the past 200 years)
- ▶ ***Fortress at Jabrin.*** Jabrin (built by Bilarub bin Sultan in 1688)
- ▶ ***Rustaq Fort.*** Rustaq (said to be built by the Persians in A.D. 600)
- ▶ ***Nizwa Fort.*** Nizwa (completed by 1680 by Sultan bin Saif)

**Industry:** The oil industry provides much of Oman's income, but most people still farm and fish for a living. The most important crops are alfalfa, bananas, coconuts, dates, and limes. Fishing crews catch sardines, rock cod, and snapper.

**Currency:** The monetary unit is the Omani rial (RO). In 1999, RO1 = U.S. $2.60.

Windtowers

A carved wooden door,
Rustaq Fort

Brothers

| | | |
|---|---|---|
| **Weights and measures:** | Metric system | |
| **Literacy:** | 59% | |
| **Local terms:** | *aflaj* | network of water channels for irrigation |
| | *Bedouin* | nomadic people of the interior Arabian peninsula |
| | *bin*, also *ibn* | "son of "; *bint* means "daughter of " |
| | *caliph* | a religious leader |
| | *dish-dasha* | a simple, long-sleeved robe worn by men |
| | *halwah* | a sweet made of sugar, water, spices, nuts, and butter |
| | *imam* | a religious leader of Islam, similar to a caliph |
| | *khawa* | Omani coffee |
| | *khanjar* | curved dagger |
| | *majlis* | meeting hall or legislative assembly |
| | *salah* | prayer |
| | *souk* | traditional market |
| | *wali* | governor or district leader |
| | *wilayat* | regional subdivision presided over by a wali |

**Famous Omanis:**

Nasir bin Murshid      (17th century)
*Political leader*

Sultan bin Saif      (? –1718)
*Political leader*

Ahmad bin Said      (?–1783)
*Political leader*

Sultan Said bin Taimur      (1910–1972)
*Political leader*

Sultan Qaboos bin Said      (1940–  )
*Political leader*

# To Find Out More

## Nonfiction

▶ Clapp, Nicholas. *The Road to Ubar: Finding the Atlantis of the Sands.* Boston: Houghton Mifflin, 1998.

▶ Dutton, Roderick. *An Arab Family.* Minneapolis: Lerner, 1985.

▶ Foster, Leila Merrell. *Saudi Arabia.* Danbury, Conn.: Children's Press, 1993.

▶ Harik, Ramsay M., and Elsa Marsten. *Women in the Middle East: Tradition and Change.* Danbury, Conn.: Franklin Watts, 1996.

▶ Jacobsen, Peter Otto. *A Family in the Persian Gulf.* New York: Bookwright Press, 1985.

▶ Tilley, P. F. *Oman.* Chelsea House, 1988.

## Websites

▶ **ArabicNews.com**
www.ArabicNews.com/BasicFacts.
OMAN/Basic.html
*News, background information,*
*recipes, and more on Oman*

▶ **CIA World Factbook**
http://www.odci.gov/cia/publications/
factbook/mu.html
*An excellent overview of the geography,*
*government, and economy of Oman*

▶ **Ministry of Information,**
**Sultanate of Oman**
www.omanet.com
*The official website of Oman's Ministry*
*of Information includes pages on his-*
*tory, government, culture and heritage,*
*a photo gallery, and more.*

## Embassy

▶ **Embassy of the Sultanate of Oman**
2342 Massachusetts Avenue, NW
Washington, DC 20008
(202) 387-1980

# Index

Page numbers in *italics* indicate illustrations.

# Meet the Author

Why did I want to write about Oman? Because I want to visit the country. I have been very close, with a tour of Yemen, Oman's neighbor. Also, I have traveled to many Middle Eastern countries. It is fun to go to a nation like Oman that preserves its cultural heritage, so that you can see what life was like over the centuries and what life is like now.

To find out about Oman, I visited my local library and my university library and read books about the country. I looked up the information on Oman in specialized encyclopedias about Arab leaders, the arts, and sports. Then, I checked the library's index of current articles and the websites on the Internet. I bought travel guides to the country. Finally, I paid attention to TV shows that featured Oman.

I am a lawyer, a United Methodist minister, a clinical psychologist, and a writer of children's books (listed in order of appearance in my life). Other books I have written include country books such as *Iraq, Kuwait, Saudi Arabia, Jordan, Lebanon, Afghanistan,* and *Bhutan* and biographies of Margaret Thatcher, Nien Cheng, Admiral David Farragut, Rachel Carson, and Benjamin Franklin. Books are a great way to travel the world and meet interesting people.

# Photo Credits

**Photographs ©:**

Anthony R. Dalton: 12;

Byron Augustin: spine, 2, 7 bottom, 8, 9, 14, 17, 18, 20, 22, 23, 29, 37, 43, 44, 46, 48, 50, 54, 57, 58, 60, 65 bottom, 67, 70 top, 71, 75, 78, 79, 80, 82 bottom, 84, 86, 88, 94, 96, 97, 98, 100, 101, 102, 103, 105, 106, 107, 108, 109, 110 top, 115, 117 bottom, 123, 124, 127, 130, 132 center, 132 bottom, 133 top, 133 bottom;

Christine Osborne: 26 top, 31, 35 (S. A. Molton), 52, 63 bottom, 69, 70 bottom, 72, 83, 120, 132 top;

Corbis-Bettmann: 39;

K. R. Downey Photography: 32;

National Geographic Image Collection: 30 right (Lynn Abercrombien), 25, 118 (Thomas Abercrombien), 73, 119 (Steve Raymer), 7 top, 10, 33 bottom, 34, 53, 66, 82 top, 85, 104, 131 bottom (James Stanfield);

Nik Wheeler: 112, 133 center;

Norm Whalen: 24, 36;

Panos Pictures: cover, 6, 64, 116 (Piers Benatar);

Photo Researchers: 33 top (Stephen Dalton);

Tony Stone Images: 87 (Jane Lewis);

Tor Eigeland: 30 left, 62, 63 top, 65 top, 76, 91;

TRIP: 110 bottom, 111 (J. Highet), 117 top (T. O'Brien), 16, 26 bottom, 27, 90, 131 top (N & J Wiseman);

Wolfgang Käehler: 28.

**Maps by Joe LeMonnier**